GUATEMALTECAS

GUATEMALTECAS

The Women's Movement, 1986–2003

SUSAN A. BERGER

UNIVERSITY OF TEXAS PRESS
Austin

Requests for permission to reproduce material from this work should
be sent to:
Permissions
University of Texas Press
P.O. Box 7819
Austin, TX 78713-7819
www.utexas.edu/utpress/about/bpermission.html

⊗ The paper used in this book meets the minimum requirements of
ANSI/NISO Z39.48-1992 (R1997) (Permanence of Paper).

LIBRARY OF CONGRESS CATALOGING-IN-PUBLICATION DATA

Berger, Susan A.
    Guatemaltecas : the women's movement, 1986–2003 / by Susan A.
Berger. — 1st ed.
        p.   cm.
    Includes bibliographical references and index.
    ISBN 0-292-70944-7 (cl. : alk. paper) — ISBN 0-292-71253-7 (pbk. :
alk. paper)
    1. Women's rights—Guatemala.   2. Women—Guatemala—Social
conditions.   3. Women—Guatemala—Economic conditions.   I. Title.
HQ1236.5.G9B47   2006
305.42′097281—dc22
2005000375

For Christina

CONTENTS

ACKNOWLEDGMENTS

In writing this book, I have accrued enormous debts. To the many Guatemaltecas who shared their knowledge and insights with me, I am eternally thankful. This book could not have been written without them. I hope that I have appropriately represented their struggles and not abused their trust. I am particularly thankful to Carmen Lucía Pellecer and Olga Rivas, who both spent considerable time helping me to understand the complexities of the Guatemalan women's movement. I am also grateful to Claudia Acevedo, Laura Asturias, Giovanna Lemus, María Morales Jorge, Sandra Morán, Noraida Ponce, Vivian Rivas, and Edna Rodríguez for their candid comments and exchanges. Without Carolina Escobar Sarti's friendship and assistance, this book would have taken longer than it did to complete, and it would have been lacking in critical ways.

I am also grateful for the institutional support of Fordham University. A faculty fellowship in the fall of 2003 provided me with the necessary time to finish the manuscript. I have also been lucky to have a group of thoughtful and skeptical students at Fordham with whom to discuss gender and Latin American politics. In addition, the Guatemala Scholars Network has provided me the necessary spaces within which to discuss shared interest in Guatemala.

Many colleagues have read earlier portions of chapter drafts. Lourdes Benería, Susan Eckstein, Linda Green, Amy Lind, Fawzia Mustafa, Mary Weismantel, and Timothy Wickham-Crowley all read parts along the way. I deeply appreciate their thoughtful comments. I am especially grateful to Norma Stoltz Chinchilla for her careful reading of the entire manuscript. Her suggestions were indispensable, as were those of another anonymous reader for the University of Texas Press. My thanks also to Theresa May at the University of Texas Press for so skillfully shepherding the manuscript through the publication process.

Finally, I owe my deepest thanks to Christina Argueta, Mali Berger, Walter Berger, and Fawzi Mustafa. I hope that each knows how grateful I am for absolutely everything.

GUATEMALTECAS

Además de cuestionar a las instituciones sociales, las diferentes
corrientes feministas están confrontando los espacios globales y
locales en los cuales nos desenvolvemos.[1]

—IRMALICIA VELÁSQUEZ NIMATUJ, GUATEMALTECA,
K'ICHE', ANTHROPOLOGIST

After more than thirty years of military rule, civilians returned to power in Guatemala in 1986. A neoliberal globalization project has accompanied the democratization process, and both have led Guatemalan women, collectively and individually, to renegotiate their positions and relations within their private and public spheres. While democratization has universally opened political space to more diverse discourses, it has particularly animated the women's movement to initiate and conduct debates over their political representation, citizenship, and engagement with the state, and the definition and priority of women's interests. Consequently, while globalization—based on the liberal ethos—is restructuring the economic participation, needs, and goals of Guatemaltecas, it is also helping to reshape the way the women's movement does politics. Shifting from protest politics to women helping women, the movement has progressively NGO-ized, professionalized, and self-authorized with legal breakthroughs.

Democratization and global restructuring have influenced the character, structure, and strategic formations of the women's movement, but the movement itself has, in turn, affected political and economic restructuring in Guatemala. Through multiple and hybrid spaces, women have pressured for the insertion of gender sensitivity into the national consciousness. They have fought for institutional reforms, employment options and conditions, social conditions, and property rights based on gender equity. In renegotiating gender positions, Guatemaltecas—though not always achieving their multiple, diverse, and, at times, contradictory ends—have highlighted issues of gender within the nationalist discourse and its policymaking apparatus.

This study undertakes an examination of the formation and practice of the Guatemalan women's movement since 1986, the manner in which it has negotiated and continues to negotiate global restructurings, and how it inserts itself institutionally and discursively into the national body politic. It explores the changing relations of power and gender and the manner in which domination has [re]configured them, and looks at how the interactive nature of politics blends with the discursive [re]imaginings of gender under global restructuring. Three hypotheses are explored in this study. First, neoliberal democratization has led to the institutionalization and NGOization of the women's movement and encouraged it to turn from protest politics to policy work and to become the helpmate of the state in imposing its neoliberal agenda. Second, while the influences of dominant global discourses are quite apparent, local definitions of femininity, sexuality, and gender equity and rights have been critical to shaping the form, content, and objectives of the women's movement in Guatemala. Third, a counterdiscourse to globalization is slowly emerging from within the women's movement that incorporates a rejection of separating production from social reproduction, while calling for the formation of strategic unity based on diverse conceptions of gender.

The study thus addresses manifold complexities informing the development of the women's movement in postwar Guatemala. In doing so, it attempts to explore and challenge the viability of using primarily northern social movement, feminist, and globalization discourses to study southern countries like Guatemala.[2] Does globalization really create favorable conditions for the growth of civil society and the weakening of authoritarian control? Does social movement development necessarily strengthen civil society and build democracy? Do autonomously organized women's groups better address the interests of women than mixed-gender organizations? Are women's strategic and practical interests truly separate and distinct? Is neoliberal restructuring presenting the conditions by which women can liberate themselves from patriarchal restrictions, or is it helping to reconfigure and ultimately strengthen the patriarchy?

SOCIAL MOVEMENTS, DEMOCRATIZATION, AND GLOBALIZATION

Much that has been written about "new" social movements in Latin America during the last fifteen years is pertinent to this study of the Guatemalan women's movement. When social movements were first spotted on the Latin American landscape, the responses of pro-democratic activists and academics alike were almost unanimously positive. It was argued that the new movements would reinvigorate civil society and advance the conception of democracy by decentering politics and political power. By demanding recognition of the rights of the previously marginalized, movements would ultimately change how politics was done.[3]

The social movements' paradigm that emerged contended that the "new" social movements were a radically different form of collective action, since they focused on issues of social norms, collective identity, and expanding the space for social expression, *not* on taking state control. Collective struggles thus became critical "wars of interpretation,"[4] clashes over the imposition of the state's postindustrial cultural model at the expense of other "local" models. It was argued that social movements had "a level of self-reflection" that changed the "loci and stakes of struggles that correspond to the emergence of a new societal type."[5] Consequently, politics was deemed relative, and social action could no longer "be seen as the result of some metasocial principle—god, tradition, the state—but society is the result of a set of systems of action involving actors who may have conflictual interests but who share certain cultural orientations."[6] These actors were perceived to be authentic representatives of interests and peoples previously marginalized by less-than-democratic states. In these analytical constructs, the women's movement was uncritically praised for building a collective consciousness, breaking down the public-private divide, and restructuring a social norm of gender equity.

These early analyses often tended to idealize the actuality of social movements while minimizing the prowess of the state, so anxious were the observers to find an alternative to the exclusionary authoritarian regimes in power throughout Latin America. As David Slater contends, "not infrequently civil society has been essentialized in a positive frame, as the terrain of the good and the enlightened."[7] In reality, however, as the Guatemalan case will show, civil society is much more complex, fragmented hierarchically by race, ethnicity, gender, and class. Neither individuals nor collectives enter the playing field on equal footing. Sonia Alvarez, Evelina Dagnino, and Arturo Escobar concur: "Civil society is a terrain mined by unequal relations of power wherein some actors gain greater access to power, as well as differential access to material, cultural and political resources, than others."[8] These power inequities fragment civil society, making it difficult for social movements to construct and sustain collective political identities. Divisive struggles occur over questions such as Who has the right to define or speak for a community? Who will set community goals? and Who will organize community activist strategies? Consequently, studies need to—and this one on Guatemala does—examine the dual nature of social movements: their embeddedness in and reconfiguration of local, national, and international power constructions.

Since the 1980s, the expansion and contradictions of globalization have also prompted a critical review of earlier idealizations of social movements. On the one hand, globalization appears to be opening up new possibilities for social activism. It facilitates the exchange of information, promotes global networks, and can initiate new forms of progressive coalitional struggles. On the other hand, globalization necessitates political reforms that can weaken and displace social movements. As we will see in later chapters, both of these trends—political opening for social activism and movement weakening—have been apparent in the Guatemalan case.

Next, broadly speaking, neoliberalism seeks to redefine the state and citizenship to better suit global free trade. Ironically, feminists note that neoliberal discourse feminizes the state, which is "represented as a drag on the global economy that must be subordinated and minimized."[9] In fact, neoliberalism reconfigures the state as the helpmate of global capital, that is, as a technical manager to ensure "the free movement of capital and goods, unrestricted labor markets, responsible banking systems, stable monetary policies, limited fiscal policies, attractive investment opportunities, and political stability."[10] In rejecting the Keynesian state model, neoliberal discourse returns to a portrayal of the state as a disinterested administrator; it is "an arena where interests are actively constructed rather than given and where power is relational."[11]

The neoliberal model thus calls for a reconceptualization of citizenship. Unlike the "passive" citizen associated with the post–World War II period, neoliberal citizens—or, to coin a term, *neocitizens*—are defined in the context of "market rationality, individual choice, personal responsibility, control over one's own fate and self-development."[12] Neocitizens, the argument goes, must become individualistic, self-sufficient, and self-motivated, and thus no longer in need of the state's safety net. They should be participatory, in a procedural way, and the model encourages citizens to work with and within the state toward nation—and institution—building. However, as we will see with the Guatemalan experience, and as Veronica Schild puts it, a necessary caution needs to be issued, because "neoliberal modernizations, as hegemonic projects, ensnare social subjects, make them act as agents and hence implicate them in their own unfolding (new) subjectivities."[13] This is not to disavow political agency but to recognize the critical connection between the rise of political identities and the state "in contexts shaped by conflict and unequal power relations."[14] These relationships become clear when we discuss the NGO-ization, legalization, and professionalization of the women's movement in Guatemala that coincided with the political and economic reforms implemented after the war.

Studying women in Guatemala also allows for a productive interrogation of gender and globalization. Gender's role as a "boundary ma[r]ker and identity producer," in fact, makes it critical to the globalizing goal of reconfiguring citizenship.[15] If women and men are to enter the economy in nontraditional ways—as global restructuring requires—then "restructuring entails reworkings on the boundaries between and meanings of femininity and masculinity, which are intimately related to the shifting boundaries and meanings of private and public, domestic and international, and local and global."[16] Globalization thus opens up discursive and institutional spaces on multiple fronts to groups struggling for gender regime reconfiguration. Women in Guatemala and elsewhere have fought within these spaces to insert gender into legislative and policy debates. At the same time, powerful globalizing forces—including local, national, and international private and public sectors—have found women, positioned as they are within the patriarchy, to be convenient envoys of restructuring in their roles as mothers, health care providers, teachers, social workers, and heads of households. "Today, women as agents are at the heart of the efforts to transform those who are 'excluded' from the benefits of an empowered life in the market into active, responsible citizens."[17] Yet case studies have detailed the many devastating impacts—impoverishment, deteriorating health, a rise in domestic violence, decreasing educational opportunities—globalization has had on Latin American women. This has led some researchers to contend that women may inadvertently be helping globalization reproduce and intensify gendered relations of domination.[18] Although some studies are less pessimistic, most, including this one, agree with Jane H. Bayes, Mary E. Hawkesworth, and Rita Mae Kelly that "the impact of globalization on women throughout the world has been as negative and undemocratic as it has been positive and liberating."[19]

In critical ways, then, we can see that the discourses of neoliberalism and social movements have come together around citizenship, identity, and participation, creating odd bedfellows. As Veronica Schild notes, there is a

convergence in form and context of different practices: legacy of the practices of social movements which highlighted identity and argued that citizenship should matter; civil governments legitimizing their public and social politics in terms of a discourse of modernity pivoting on the key issues of autonomy, accountability and responsibility; growing trend in international aid to bolster democratic politics in the region by emphasizing decentralization and active (economic) citizenship.[20]

Some would argue, as I do in the Guatemalan case, that neoliberalism has discursively pilfered the concerns of social movements as a means of maintaining stability and state control over civil society. A democratic façade not only provides the state with international legitimacy, but it encourages—at least for a while—social movement activists to work with and within the state to achieve so-called common goals while simultaneously allowing the state to withdraw from servicing society. Civil society, thus, in the words of George Yúdice, "has a double origin: in neoliberalism's need for stability and political legitimation and in grassroots organization for the state of survival in the face of structural adjustment."[21]

Nongovernmental organizations (NGOs) play an increasingly important intermediary role between the state and civil society in global restructuring. As we will see in Guatemala, the withdrawal of the neoliberal state from servicing civil society has led NGOs to step in to attend to previously accepted public-sector tasks. They have helped to provide social services to the poor; manage environmentally protected areas; run homeless and domestic violence shelters; provide educational and health services; and build, expand, and improve basic infrastructure. In addition, NGOs have become important sources of employment for local professionals while also providing discursive and ideological orientations under the guise of individual rights to populations destabilized by restructuring.

The growing importance of NGOs has not been without its problems and critics. Many argue that within the conditions of global restructuring, social movements have NGOized in order to obtain international funding. While allowing groups to upscale, the funding has left them vulnerable to donor discipline and political strategies and has pushed groups to formalize structures, decision-making channels, communications, and relations with the state. Sonia Alvarez and others have concluded that these changes are reshaping Latin American women's activist groups, and this study concurs. Alvarez writes:

> The NGO boom of the 1990s is marked by a region-wide shift away from feminist activities centered on popular education, mobilization, and poor and working-class women's empowerment and a move toward policy-focused activities, issue-specialization, and resource concentra-

tion among the more technically adept, transnationalized and professionalized NGOs within the feminist field.[22]

The political implications of these developments are far-reaching. According to the social movement literature, the organization of civil society will force state accountability. However, the NGOization of social movements may unintentionally shelter the state from public discontent by "helping to buttress a public sector evacuated by the state and at the same time making it possible for the state to steer clear of what was once seen as its responsibility."[23] The state may become more distant and protected from civil society as local populations expect less from the state and more from nongovernmental sectors. If the state is sheltered from public discontent, it stands to reason that state institutions and policymakers will feel less responsible to civil society. This may lead to less rather than more democracy as the state focuses on managing, rather than providing for, civil society while keeping governability foremost in consideration. Other studies will be needed before making pronouncements one way or the other, but this study starts the process of closely examining whether or not NGOs of Guatemaltecas aid in the building and strengthening of local civil societies and what political consequences have occurred from NGOs acting as intermediaries between the state and civil society.

A related concern of NGOization is the internationalizing of local movements, which refers both to the ability of local movements to use the global communications network to exchange information and build cross-border networks, and to the influence of international funding and cultures on local movements. Although most academics and activists argue that the building of international social movement networks can be crucial in pressuring oppressive local governments for change, they are also wary of the undue effect the international can have on the construction of local interests and organizations. We must thus ask questions such as: How does the goal of international dissemination affect the types and goals of information communicated? What effect does the possible "imbrication of the transnational and the grassroots (most evident in the action of NGOs)" have on local cultural reproduction?[24] and How do international donors help to (re)shape local interests, the expression of demands, political strategies, and structures?

At the same time, while it is clear that globalization is forcing changes on women and women's organizing in Guatemala and Latin America, some feminists contend that it may also ultimately present the basis for building feminist solidarity across borders. For some, this solidarity is more or less essentialized from shared oppressions ("all women suffer under globalization and thus must unite"), but for Chandra Talpade Mohanty the anti-globalization movement becomes a much broader, more militant feminist cause of solidarity founded upon difference. This requires making strategic and tactical alliances with and between groups involved in local place-based civic activism and connecting them with the larger anti-globalization struggles while simultaneously rethinking "patriarchies and hegemonic masculinities in relation to present day globalization and nationalisms."[25] Charlotte Hooper also moves in this direction by showing the discursive links between feminism, women of the South, and globalization in her analysis of globalization narratives as "rape scripts."[26] She cites, among others, a 1994 article in *The Economist* on Myanmar entitled "Ripe for Rape":

> Asia's businessmen have had their eyes on Myanmar's rich resources for a while. Unlike most of its neighbors, it still has teak forests to be felled and its gem deposits are barely exploited. Its natural beauties and its astonishing Buddhist architecture make it potentially irresistible to tourists . . . Businessmen are beginning to take the first steps towards exploiting this undeveloped land.[27]

As Hooper observes, "The reader is metaphorically invited to identify with the foreign (Western) businessmen hoping to rape this pubescent girl with her unexploited gems and irresistible natural beauties. This imagery draws directly on racist and sexist colonial discourse about White male exploration of and adventure in 'virgin territories.'"[28] Through the rape script analogy, Hooper makes just the kind of linkage between North/ South and gender/globalization that Mohanty is asking feminists to make in critiquing globalization and building North/South feminist solidarity within the anti-globalization struggles. She, like Mohanty, links the building of feminist solidarity to knowledge and critical awareness of difference, rather than to essentialist identity. The goal thus becomes to build a counterdiscourse to globalization, a move that some Guatemalan women activists are also beginning to undertake.

Issues of identity are also keenly embedded in any reading of the Guatemalan women's movement. Many activists and scholars alike contend that identity construction is one of the most contested concepts of social movement formation. Studies of social movements tend to split between those that explain collective "action in terms of structural opportunities, leadership, and ideological and organizational networks" and those interested in the "construction, contestation, and negotiation of collective identities in the process of political activity."[29] While some identity theorists lean toward essentialist interpretations, most view identity as "constructed in action"; collective identity is "built through interactions, negotiation, and relationships with the environment."[30] This identity is in constant flux as it responds to the needs, demands, and interests of participants who are themselves responding within local, national, and international contexts. Thus, as Lynn Stephen notes, "the very nature of the phenomena we study, the collective identity of social movements is a 'moving target,' with different definitions predominating at different points in a movement career."[31]

The formation, mobilization, and maintenance of collective identity have become concerns of feminist activists and will be explored here in the Guatemalan case. Why do women organize? What binds them together collectively in political action? How does identity affect mobilization, organization, strategies, and tactics? In the mid-1980s, Maxine Molyneux, writing about Nicaragua and critiquing calls for biologically founded universal sisterhood, argued that women's interests are "historically and culturally constituted" and loosely divided between practical and strategic interests. Practical interests refer to women's immediate needs and demands for better housing, work conditions, social services, and the like. Strategic interests refer to gender equity demands. According to Molyneux, "In the formulation of practical interests there is the assumption that there is compliance with the existing gender order, while in the case of strategic interests there is an explicit questioning of that order and of the compliance of some women with it."[32] Molyneux's analysis opened the floodgate to the interest paradigm debate. Some worried that her analysis set up a hierarchy of interests, privileging strategic feminist interests over women's practical needs–based interests.[33] Others noted that the practical-strategic distinction, as outlined, erroneously creates a rigid binary—an either-or—situation. Still others concluded that the analysis disregards agency and obscures difference, relegating women's collective interests to structural determinism and at times to essentialism.[34]

While Molyneux has argued that some of the criticisms are inappropriately based on misunderstanding and oversimplification of her original comments made specifically on the Nicaraguan case, the debate—misunderstandings and all—has sharpened our critical "interest" eye. Lynn Stephen, for example, has noted that "women's participation in alternative political organizations operating in public spaces can be seen as part of a larger social search for identity and the appropriation of a cultural field with the objective of obtaining the right to be different."[35] On the other hand, Anna Jonasdottir has suggested that we distinguish between needs and interests.[36] "Needs are assumed to exist, while interests have to be articulated and are therefore willed." As Shirin Rai notes, however, both needs and interests are location situated: "[I]ssues of class, religion, and ethnicity all impinge upon and disturb this category."[37] Meanwhile, Gayatri Spivak has suggested that we think in terms of strategic interest formulations, emphasizing individual and collective agencies.[38] In thinking about the Guatemalan women's movement, categories like the strategic and the practical, as well as needs and interests, do help analysts to more fully consider the diversity of women's lives, interests, and actions. Still, as we observe in the next chapter, the division between strategic and practical interests is rather opaque, and the defining of needs and interests is often a complex process heavily influenced by external factors.

Embedded in the interest debate, but not necessarily always articulated by it, is the concept of empowerment. Widely used by activists, World Bank policymakers, and state agencies alike, empowerment has become an embattled and clichéd concept. Feminists of the South first started using the word in the 1970s and 1980s primarily to tackle gender differences in resource management and distribution. While power relations were inherent in these analyses—asking who controls and decides who gets what resources—in practice, empowerment strategies often stressed the systemic inclusion of women rather than questioning patriarchal power structures. In the 1990s, the notion of empowerment was expanded to emphasize and work toward the dismantling of power inequities. Symptomatic of this new usage is Srilatha Batliwala's definition:

> Empowerment is manifested as a redistribution of power, whether between nations, classes, castes, races, genders, or individuals. The goals of women's empowerment are to challenge patriarchal ideology (male domination and women's subordination); to transform the structures and institutions that reinforce and perpetuate gender discrimination and social inequality (the family, caste, class, religion, educational processes, and institutions, the media, health practices and systems, laws and civil codes, political processes, development models, and government institutions); and to enable poor women to gain access to, and control of, both material and informational resources."[39]

Some have argued that the concept continues to be culturally bound within Western individualism. Still, many feminists of the South—including Guatemala—and the North agree on the desired multiple ends of empowerment while disagreeing on the means to those ends. Will organizational, structural, or policy changes actually empower or disempower women? What kinds of organizations better empower women? Do institutional reforms empower some women and disempower others? How do race, ethnicity, and class impact empowering processes and outcomes? Do legislative reforms alter or cloak power inequities? Supporters of an empowerment political strategy note that though empowerment is gradual, nonlineal, and multidimensional, there also is no "straightforward cause and effect relationship between process and outcomes."[40] If this is the case, does the empowerment paradigm lose its purpose on a feminist agenda? If activists cannot reasonably determine the outcome of strategies designed to empower, do they sometimes unwittingly contribute to the disempowerment of women? Or, conversely, does the recognition of the complexity of the relationship between empowerment processes and objectives lead activists to become more sensitive to social variants?

Empowerment advocates within and outside Guatemala often cite organizational structure as key to the empowering process. They argue that women's interests will best be served by autonomous, nonhierarchical organizations in which women organize themselves, set organizational goals, and determine struggles and strategies. Autonomous organizing frees women from subordination to political parties, unions, movements, and agencies while providing them with the structural facility within which to construct, articulate, and struggle for gendered identities and interests. Additionally, it is argued, organizing in a nonhierarchical manner encourages the building of a participatory democratic political culture and the capacitation of all participants.

The Guatemalan case, however, concurs with other studies that have shown that organizational structure does not necessarily enhance the feminist cause. Molyneux notes,

> [E]ven when women do organize autonomously, they do not always act collectively in pursuit of their gender interests. Women's interests cannot "be read off" from the organizational form in which they are expressed; the mere fact of an organization's autonomy or internal organizational structure does not indicate that it is a privileged vehicle for the expression of women's interests or, indeed, that it is entirely free from authority, either internally with respect to the organization concerned or with regard to external influence.[41]

A so-called autonomous organization does not exist within an isolation tank, cut off from power incongruities within. Molyneux continues, "Thus while not recognizing a 'higher authority' it might recognize an authority in the form of a privileged interpretation of reality."[42] Clearly the complex intersections of class, ethnicity, race, sexual orientation, and geography cannot be ignored when delving into institution/organization studies, and Guatemala is no exception.

Many feminists of the South have long insisted that class, race, ethnicity, sexual orientation, and geography separate women organizationally, both in their definitions of themselves and in the construction of their interests. They question whether gender can be a sufficient basis for politics and if gender really has an "imperial grasp on the psyche."[43] Many maintain that "women's emancipation is bound up with the fate of the larger community"[44] and thus have encouraged women's movements to join with a larger struggle for social justice and human rights. Practically, this has meant that women have joined collective actions—those whose goals and strategies are "manned" from the outside—and made associational linkages, in which women's organizations decide to link up with other political organizations. Women have expressed dissatisfaction with the results of both strategies, however, and thus continue to think through the relationships between identity, organizational formats, and political strategies. Like women throughout the South, Guatemalan women are also grappling with these issues: Is it possible for indigenous and mestiza women to join forces and work within the state for gender-specific reforms? Can activist women simultaneously wear two hats, one feminist and the other bureaucratic? How can professional urban women represent poor rural women in organizing and reform-making endeavors? What kind of feminist unity can be built from within a nation that is grossly polarized along ethnic and class lines?

THE GUATEMALAN WOMEN'S MOVEMENT

In the following chapters, I offer a case study of the Guatemalan women's movement in an effort to better understand it, as well as the construction, objectives, and operations of social movements within a globalizing context. Although the Guatemalan women's movement has its roots in violence, it nevertheless developed within the political and economic global restructuring that took place in Guatemala after 1985. Between 1978 and 1985 the military state destroyed approximately 626 villages and disappeared or killed some 200,000 Guatemalans; the violence displaced more than 1.5 million and drove more than 150,000 into refugee camps in Mexico. Approximately 83 percent of the victims were Maya and 17 percent were mestizo.[45] Responding to state violence and to the economic crisis that accompanied it, Guatemalan women—indigenous and mestiza, poor and rich, rural and urban—joined mixed-gendered social justice organizations to defend their so-called practical rights "to the resources and services necessary for their traditional gender roles in production and reproduction."[46] Consequently, they demanded to know the whereabouts of disappeared husbands, fathers, and children; decried forced military recruitment; called for land for the dispossessed; organized cooperatives to better feed their families; and joined armed revolutionary groups. Most of the women and the organizations they joined did not actively question the patriarchal order or pursue gender equality. Their focus on social justice and human rights, however, did ultimately help to destabilize public and private gender regimes.

In 1986, the military—pressured by a sagging economy, the failure of its modernization development policies, growing popular discontent, and the international community—returned power to civilian rule.[47] A new constitution promised the democratization of the state and civil society. In 1996, the government signed peace accords with the leftist guerrillas, the Unidad Revolucionaria Nacional Guatemalteca (Guatemalan National Revolutionary Union, URNG), officially ending the civil war that had scorched Guatemala for over thirty years. The state appeared to commit itself to finding new ways, other than violence, by which to define its relationship with civil society. These political reforms were essential to and inseparable from the government's larger global restructuring project that includes the liberalization of trade, the privatization of state industries, the "rationalization" of economic production, and the implementation of the Puebla-Panama Plan and the Central American Free Trade Agreement (CAFTA).[48]

The rising influence of international feminism on development and regional discourses within this atmosphere of global restructuring encouraged some Guatemalan women to demand inclusion in the democratization and economic restructuring processes. They insisted on their participation in the peace accords, called for legislative and educational reforms to enhance gender equality, held forums on domestic violence and the rights of women workers, fought for the engendering of state policymaking, and lobbied for the establishment of women's studies programs in the universities. To achieve these goals, women formed autonomous organizations often supported by international nongovernmental organizations and funds, entered into strategic alliances with other political groups, and worked within and in cooperation with state agencies. Many women continued to work in mixed-gender-directed collectives, but established women's committees within the organizations to better respond to the needs and demands of female members.

By the late 1990s, it appeared as if women and women's organizations in Guatemala had succeeded in creating a "movement."[49] In addition, Guatemalteca activists looked as if they were moving from being women involved in organizations fighting for social justice to women organizing women to fight for social justice *and* gender equality. The reality of the Guatemalan women's movement is not quite so linear, however. A closer analysis reveals the contradictory nature of women's collective action under global restructuring. Factionalism, clientelism, NGOization, and institutionalization all plague the movement, making common interest formation, goal setting, and united action arduous. Global restructuring has encouraged both the movement and the state to reimagine the Other (and themselves in relation to the Other). This has led to the construction of new institutional arrangements, political identities, and discourses, some of which have undoubtedly empowered women and others that have grossly or subtly disempowered them. During these processes, Guatemaltecas, at times, have challenged "domination as a particular 'congealed' structure of power relations and oppressive exclusionary identities," but, at other times, they have participated in "the emergence and development of new forms of domination."[50]

ORGANIZATION OF THIS STUDY

The remainder of the book is divided into five chapters based on research trips of varying lengths to Guatemala between 1996 and 2002. On these trips I interviewed women activists, government officials, academics, and journalists; researched materials produced by various organizations; kept up with mainstream publications as they related to women and gender issues; and used the small but rich resources of the documentation center of the feminist nongovernmental organization Agrupación de Mujeres Tierra Viva.

A cautionary note should be made about the study at this point. While ethnicity, class, and geographical location remain crucial to understanding Guatemalan politics and society today, most of the primary research of the study was conducted with women living at the time of the interviews in Guatemala City. To counter this urban bias, I did several things. First, in arranging the interviews, I tried to be as inclusive of difference as possible. Thus, those interviewed in Guatemala City were both of rural and urban origin; temporary and long-term residents of the city; rich, middle class, and poor; indigenous and mestiza. Second, I rely on the rich testimonial and ethnographic literature of rural Guatemala to flush out some urban/rural differences.

Still, my decision to concentrate on interviewing women activists primarily in the capital city was movement driven. The Guatemalan women's movement is not by any means solely an urban movement, but much of its administration is urban centered, and ties to the rural sector are tenuous at times. The reasons for this are complicated and will be discussed in the next chapter but clearly relate to issues of the NGOization, institutionalization, and professionalization of women's organizations that have been prompted by neoliberalism.

Guatemaltecas have long been pushed to the background, not only in domestic Guatemalan politics but also in academic analyses of all kinds. A basic objective of this study is to begin the process of moving women and considerations of gender to the forefront by engendering political analysis of Guatemala. Chapters 2 through 5 explore the ways in which the theoretical topics introduced in this first chapter—the institutionalization of social movements, the essentialization and strategic construction of identity to achieve political objectives, debates between international and local discourses of gender, and the means to empowerment—have resonated within the Guatemalan women's movement. Chapter 2 centers our attention on Guatemaltecas as political actors. In tracing the evolution of the women's movement in Guatemala, the chapter exposes the interlocked relationship between material needs and strategic interests. It also explores the associations between local and global variables in shaping the trajectory of the women's movement in Guatemala and examines the ways in which women have inserted themselves into the ongoing processes of democratization and globalization. Their participation has by no means been linear, nor has it been unproblematic, and the case shows similarities with those of other regional social movements in recent years.

Chapter 3 illustrates the elasticity of patriarchal norms, despite the growth of the organizational and institutional participation of women. The law has become a site of contestation between the state and women in attempts by each to redefine citizenship and gender. Although legislative reforms enacted since 1986 have diminished the legal bases for gender discrimination, they have not necessarily weakened patriarchal institutions and practices. A close reading of the laws and the debates surrounding them points to some of the concrete ways patriarchy has continued to perpetuate itself even in the midst of institutional reforms. This discussion of the relationship between reform and continuity leads to an examination of the debate over organizational autonomy and institutionalization and analyzes the benefits Guatemalan women do and do not obtain from institutional participation.

Chapter 4 discusses the ways in which identity can be constructed and utilized for political purposes. In particular, the chapter focuses on the construction of a lesbian political identity in Guatemala and reveals some of the ways in which identity construction is complicated by competing local and global discourses, traditions, and constraints built around sexuality. In addition, the chapter explores how power differentials between movement activists representing a variety of identity questions and definitions have played a part in focusing, refocusing, and checking movement energy and direction. The chapter clearly points to potential problems of basing political action on a shared identity; most notably it demonstrates a tendency to marginalize the alternative experiences and histories of sexual minorities in Guatemala. Still, identity politics as employed by Guatemalteca lesbians has helped to introduce sexual politics into the political agenda in Guatemala and has opened a needed debate and discussion of sexuality.

Chapter 5 examines the ways in which globalization both encourages the rethinking of gender regimes and simultaneously depends on traditional patriarchal structures. As women have entered the formal economy, mainly as machinists in apparel and textile *maquilas*,[51] they have been both welcomed and disapproved of by their families, fellow male workers and unionists, and employers. Practically, families recognize their need for the salaries of women, union leaders understand the benefits of organizing female workers, and employers know that their profit margins depend on the cheap labor of their female employees. At the same time, families, male-dominated unions, and employers all want and need to keep ideal gender norms in place that subordinate women to male privilege. The chapter discusses the inherent instability of the system and examines the varied ways in which Guatemaltecas have responded to and reshaped structures and discourses in attempts to ensure that their diverse needs as women and workers are met within the globalizing economy.

Chapter 6 returns to some of the key topics of concern introduced in the study: gendered collective identity formation, interest articulation, and empowerment at the intersection of the local and the global. What spaces is the neoliberal/democratic order opening to women in Guatemala? What spaces are being closed? Are global identities replacing or eroding local ones, or are local sexual identities molding global discourses for local consumption? Is NGOization and institutionalization providing critical structural support for the women's movement, or is it threatening its very existence? How are Guatemaltecas using counterdiscourses to empower themselves collectively and individually?

This study does not pretend to answer any of these questions in either a definitive or comprehensive manner, but it does hope to establish a foundation on which future research and discussion of gender politics in Guatemala can proceed. In doing so, I hope that the study will encourage others to do further research to engender the study of Guatemalan politics and make more visible the diversity of Guatemalteca political participation.

INSIDE (AND) OUT:
HOME, WORK, AND ORGANIZING

Chapter 2

No se oyen
pero escuchan.
Están sentadas en la parte de atrás.
Cuando por fin alzan la mano,
descubren el rostro
de una palabra
con ojos de liebre asustada
que huye
de las cocinas
de los cuartos
y las salas
para asomarse
—aunque sea por un instante—
a un lugar sin paredes
pero con alma.[1]

—CAROLINA ESCOBAR SARTI, "LAS MUJERES NO SE OYEN"

Beginning in the late 1970s, Guatemaltecas started to participate in social movements in relatively large numbers for the first time. Social, economic, and political variables had historically divided, isolated, restricted, and subordinated women in Guatemala, making it difficult for them to build a strategically imagined community based on gender. But in the late 1970s, the confluence of a number of domestic and international factors not only opened up new political spaces to women but also encouraged women to think about gender as a basis for identity politics. Guatemaltecas took advantage of these changes, struggling to fashion and expand spaces to best address their multiple needs and desires as individuals, classes, ethnic groups, and, for the first time, as women.

To begin to understand the unfolding Guatemalan story, this chapter looks at two founding elements: the strategies and tactics used to build—and the difficulties of doing so—a united political community around gender, and the multiple political implications of changing gender norms. The chapter looks at why the women's movement developed when it did and in the ways it did; how Guatemaltecas have defined their interests and needs within or outside the women's movement; in what ways the movement has been inclusive and exclusive; how women's organizations have negotiated the socioeconomic and political realities of democratization and economic restructuring; and how the state and the movement have interacted. The chapter reveals the actuality of the close relationship between practical and strategic interests, as well as the dialectics between neoliberal reforms and the institutionalization of the women's movement in Guatemala.

ANTECEDENTS TO THE GUATEMALAN WOMEN'S MOVEMENT

Although the growth of the women's movement is a fairly recent occurrence in Guatemala, Guatemaltecas—usually individually rather than collectively—have always participated in the nation's political and economic development: in the formal and informal markets, in class and cultural organizations, and in political struggles. Indigenous and mestiza women were active in the anticolonial struggles of the late eighteenth and early nineteenth centuries,[2] in the Liberal-Conservative conflicts in the early part of the twentieth century,[3] and in the nationalist struggles of the years 1944–1954.[4] They have historically supported their families with formal and informal, salaried and unsalaried labor as domestics, agriculturalists, innkeepers, teachers, proprietors of informal *comedores* (eating establishments), marketwomen, and clerical workers. Still, women were excluded legally, economically, and as Ana Silvia Monzón asserts, within the national social imagination. Laws restricted women from acting on their own behalf judicially, they could not vote until 1945,[5] and a woman needed the permission of her husband to work outside the home. Women were discouraged from entering certain professions, generally received less pay than their male counterparts, and had difficulty getting land titles in their names.[6]

Symbolic codes sanctioned by the Catholic Church and by civil laws held that men should protect and provide for women, and that women, in turn, should obey and serve men.[7] The female body was considered impure and women untrustworthy, necessitating the policing of the female body. Women were excluded "from public spaces, sacred activities, and rituals such as the traditional dances"[8] and supervised so as not to succumb to sensual pleasures or their "love of luxuries."[9] The social construction of femininity thus encouraged concealing middle- and upper-class mestizas behind closed doors. It simultaneously stigmatized indigenous and poor women who had to leave their homes for economic reasons while demasculinizing the men who *allowed* them to do so. In 1885, Helen Josephine Sanborn, a young American woman traveling in Guatemala, wrote:

> The streets are full of Indian women, but one sees very few of the higher classes, and this was so noticeable that we asked, "Where are the ladies of Guatemala?" and received the answer, "In their houses." It is contrary to custom and all rules of etiquette for a lady to go on the street alone, even in the daytime. She must be attended by a servant or another companion, and it is improper for ladies, even in groups of two or three, to be out after dark unattended by a servant. Ladies and gentlemen never walk together on the street unless married.[10]

The fact that poor women did not or could not uphold social norms of gender helped to justify society's discrimination against them; their presence outside the home labeled them impure, dirty, inferior, and undeserving of the respect given to "real" women, that is, middle- and upper-class mestizas. The fathers, brothers, and husbands of working women were simultaneously labeled less than men for their inability either to provide for or properly manage "their women."

Despite the historical social, political, and economic subordination of women in Guatemala, Guatemaltecas began to build a collective struggle based on diverse conceptions of gender in the late twentieth century. Why did women begin to organize at that particular historical juncture? What factors led them to begin to reevaluate and redefine dominant gender discourses and powers? How did the movement define and redefine itself, strategically playing with varied definitions of gender and citizenship?

THE BEGINNINGS: CARETAKERS AND CAREGIVERS OR FEMINISTS?

In the late 1970s and early 1980s, Guatemalan women began organizing to confront escalating state repression, the rising cost of living, and land consolidation—all of which, together with the growing number of women in the paid labor force and the increased incidence of divorce, struck at the very core of the social relations of the Guatemalan family.[11] This destabilized women's identities as both caretakers (doing the work necessary for the maintenance of the social relations of the family) and caregivers (doing the work necessary for the physical maintenance of the family).[12] These political and economic crises undermined socially constructed gender roles and identities and created the conditions for possible gender regime changes closely linking material and strategic interests.[13]

The Guatemalan state unleashed ferocious repression in the late 1970s and early 1980s in its attempts to destroy the leftist guerrilla forces by then unified under the Unidad Revolucionaria Nacional Guatemalteca (Guatemalan National Revolutionary Union; URNG)[14] and, in the eyes of some observers, to modernize the rural economy. Between 1979 and 1985, the military killed some 200,000 Guatemalans, left over 100,000 children orphaned, and forced 1.5 million citizens from their homes. In conjunction with this destruction, the state sought to reorganize and control rural community life to make it more accommodating to large-scale capitalist production. It set up strategic hamlets,[15] forced peasants to participate in civilian patrols,[16] confiscated peasant lands, and organized rural development programs under the direction of the military. This so-called modernization project, in essence, was premised upon the genocide of the indigenous populations and eradication of their cultures;[17] the vast majority of those killed during the repression were indigenous peoples, who were not allowed to openly practice their traditions in government-controlled hamlets and were forbidden to speak their native languages. Some indigenous women, like Cristina Calel, a leader of the Comité de Unidad Campesina (Committee of Peasant Unity; CUC), cut their long braided hair and stopped wearing indigenous clothing to try to disguise and ultimately protect their identities from the military.[18] The state, however, came to define indigenous culture, and thus indigenous peoples, as both politically subversive and anticapitalist.[19]

The nation also faced a severe economic depression in the late 1970s and 1980s that exacerbated already growing socioeconomic inequities of expanding capitalist modes of production in the countryside.[20] The cost of living quadrupled between 1980 and 1991 as inflation rates rose to 41% in 1990. The nation's currency, the quetzal (Q), was devalued several times, and the national debt climbed to $2.6 billion by early 1991, increasing debt service payments to one-third of the value of national exports.[21] These conditions were further aggravated by state corruption, which allowed for, among other things, the growth of more unequal forms of land distribution. For example, the military as an institution acquired land, and individual officers used their political positions in the 1970s and 1980s to amass personal wealth, with many officers obtaining land in the northern provinces. General Romeo Lucas García, who in 1977 was in charge of development in the northern section of the country known as the Northern Transversal Strip and was the minister of defense between 1975 and 1976, acquired three estates, totaling 130,000 acres. By 1979, 64.5% of the land was held by 2.5% of the population, while 97.5% of the population owned 35.5%. Women owned only 6.6% of all land in Guatemala, and 89.8% of their holdings were 7.0 hectares or less.[22]

As a result, the already poor living conditions of the majority of Guatemalans worsened. In 1980, 71.1% of the population lived in conditions of poverty, and 39.6% of that group lived in extreme poverty. Nine years later, 70% lived in poverty, and 52% of that number lived in extreme poverty. Official unemployment rose from 2.2% to 3.4% between 1980 and 1990, but these rates did not take into account fluctuations in the informal economy and underemployment. For example, underemployment rates rose from 43% to 60% between 1980 and 1990, and underemployment for indigenous women was estimated at a staggering 91% by the 1990s.

Not surprisingly, these political and economic crises created the conditions for shifting gender roles. An act of state repression could abruptly remove males from homes, extended families, and villages, leaving women alone to protect cultural traditions and provide for children and the elderly. Economic hardships required women to seek survival in nontraditional ways that did not adhere to ideal social norms of gender. The Catholic Church also encouraged women to take on new responsibilities and positions in the family and community. Vatican II had initiated a more active role for the church in the liberation of the poor and also began to encourage women to be more active in the public sphere. In the early 1970s, for instance, the church began to offer courses in social capacity, literacy training, and development to both men and women; it arranged scholarships for activists to study abroad and helped form cooperatives with male and female participants. As Catholic Action gave way to liberation theology and the formation of Christian Base Communities (Comunidades Eclesiales de Base; CEBs), hierarchical control, male dominance in the church, and charity work were all questioned, though never completely dismantled.[23] Many women benefited from these changes and became active in CEBs. María Teresa Aguilar, a member of the Permanent Commission of Guatemalan Refugees in the 1980s, remembers, "When I was nineteen, a priest sent me to Rafael Landívar University where they gave courses to train community development workers. I learned a little about that, and with the help of other *compañeros,* we set up committees. We didn't know how to go about it, but you learn by doing. That's how we got a health station . . ."[24] As the repression escalated in the late 1970s, the church lent moral, organizational, and economic support to the Guatemalan civil society when most other organizations were being forced to dismantle or go underground. For instance, the Grupo de Apoyo Mutuo (Mutual Support Group; GAM), an organization of the families of the disappeared, held its first meeting in the home of the archbishop of Guatemala.

With their caretaking and caregiving roles threatened, and the church's traditional dictates in flux in the late 1970s and early 1980s, Guatemalan women were drawn to four main types of organizations, which could be labeled primarily as practical or materialist: human rights, economic based, student, and revolutionary.[25] As their counterparts in other Latin American countries did at the same time, Guatemaltecas took a leading role in organizing human rights groups and demanding to know the fate of disappeared relatives. One such group, GAM, initially founded in 1984 by mestizas in the capital city, quickly became a more nationally representative mestizo/indigenous organization, with approximately two-thirds of its members being Maya.[26] Women were also active in the formation and activities of peasant and urban unions. For example, they participated from the beginning in the CUC, which was founded in 1978 to defend the political and economic rights of the peasantry and rural workers.[27] Other women helped to organize the Comunidades de Poblaciones en Resistencia (Communities of Populations in Resistance; CPR)—communities of individuals who had been forced to flee their villages due to state repression—and refugees in camps in Mexico. Women also joined student associations and took up arms with various revolutionary fronts, including the URNG.[28]

The organizations formed in the late 1970s and early 1980s were generally mixed gendered and initially governed by dominant gender codes.[29] Still, the very acts of women entering the public sphere in new ways called into question traditional notions of femininity and masculinity, forcing women, social movements, and eventually the entire society to confront the validity of prescribed gender roles. Prior to the late 1970s, dominant gender norms were similar to those of the eighteenth and nineteenth centuries. As Margarita, an indigenous K'iche' activist, told Norma Stoltz Chinchilla, "In the family, the man is the one who rules and brings in money, thus we (women) must serve and attend to him."[30] As we have already established, women still needed to get the permission of their fathers, husbands, and in-laws to participate in activities outside the home. Even with permission, traveling for work and being out alone, especially at night, led to questions about a woman's virtue from family members, neighbors, and the community. At the same time, economic and political conditions had changed, prompting some men to accept or even encourage their wives, daughters, and sisters to take on nontraditional roles in the public sphere. Nevertheless, in so doing they by no means sought to dismantle the patriarchal domination of the family. The experiences of Cristina Calel, a CUC activist, were not uncommon. She explained that she first began to work with social movement organizations at the urging of her husband, "At first, when my husband told me that we were going to have a meeting, I thought, 'What am I going to say? What am I going to do?' But, little by little, I adjusted and I participated with the other *compañeras*, I learned."[31] Despite his real encouragement, however, Calel's husband was typical of other men at the time, trying to direct the type and degree of her participation. She explains:

> My *compañero* helped me a lot to clarify what were the causes of our problems. For example, he asked me, "if you feel sorry for a friend who has no sweater and is cold, what would you do?" I responded that I would give her my sweater. He said that that was not the answer; that what we needed to do was to organize ourselves . . .[32]

Calel's participation and that of other women thus did not translate into an immediate concern about gender norms. Still, once involved in various organizations, women grew more politically sure of themselves; they began to analyze for themselves "the causes of their problems"[33] and demand new responsibilities and rights. This sometimes put them at odds with family and community members, pushing them to think further about their condition in the context of gender. Reflecting on her own experiences, one indigenous activist noted:

> About the reaction of my family to my political and organizing activities, the big problem occurred when I was working in community development. Probably people had always spoken badly of me. But not as much when I was a labor organizer. When I began to work with the peasant leagues. That was when I had the most problems because I had to leave the house at 4:00 A.M. in the morning—we had to visit *aldeas* that were very far away—and I would return very late at night. Therefore, people said that I was the lover of the man I worked with. And many people did not understand my work. My mother understood but not my aunts and uncles. They said that I was being compromised

by communism. They told my mother that I should quit my work because the man I worked with was a communist and was teaching me
bad things. But I was already very (politically) conscious by then. My
mother told me many times to quit work; that it was better not to continue working; that it was now time to get married . . .[34]

In addition to confronting families and communities about issues of
their femininity, women activists were also attacked by the gender-specific
state terror tactics used as an integral part of the military's counterinsurgency program.[35] Guatemaltecas were raped and sexually tortured and
degraded, reminders that they were not disembodied activists but gendered ones.[36] Yolanda Aguilar, a student and labor activist who was ar-
rested, tortured, and repeatedly raped when she was fifteen years old,
remembered:

> The rape was the most physically, morally, and psychologically diffi-
> cult . . . Under these circumstances, one cannot break with years of up-
> bringing and beliefs of what it means to be a woman. The thing that hurt
> the most was to have been dirtied by those types . . . animals, beasts.
> But worse still was to feel impotent; that was the most difficult. At first,
> I was strong enough to kick, hit, and shout . . . The first time that they
> raped me, I cried and screamed. But the second, the third, and the ones
> that followed, because there were so many times, I was simply there; a
> lump thrown on the ground.[37]

As Aguilar notes, struggles against the state, as well as the family and
community, led women to begin to question "years of upbringing and beliefs of what it means to be a woman." Thus they not only confronted
external concepts of femininity but also the internalized versions of those
norms. One activist admits that she did not want to go to night school
to finish her education because "girls end up with a baby real soon because they are out in the streets at night."[38] Likewise, Lorena, a URNG
combatant, informed Jennifer Harbury:

> It is hard to be a woman up here, yes. It's harder than I could ever begin
> to tell you, but not for the reasons you are thinking . . . The problems
> lay in my notions of what a woman should or shouldn't do, should or
> shouldn't think. These things my culture had taught me, my neighbors,
> my school mates, the people of my small *ladino* town.[39]

This combatant concludes that despite the fact that she was physically
and ideologically prepared to fight in the revolution, the internalization
of dominant gender norms made it difficult for her.

As women entered new spheres to fight for survival and for ideologically based reforms, they were thus forced to rethink questions of femininity and consequently slowly began to place questions of gender on the agendas of the social movements in which they participated.[40] Within the revolutionary forces, for example, female recruits were initially prohibited from participating in active combat and instead were relegated to performing "stakeouts, providing security for a *compañero* preparing for an operation, preparing meals while the *compañeros* worked, cleaning house—those kind of jobs." According to one URNG recruit, however, "We never accepted that. We rebelled and began to demand other kinds of responsibilities and the *compañeros* really let loose on us. They accused us of being comfortable and petit bourgeois, of not valuing domestic work— this was coming from our own *compañeros!*"[41] Over time, women revolutionaries forced their male counterparts to distribute tasks more equitably and took a more active part in the many roles of armed conflict.[42] Similar conflicts and discussions occurred in many social organizations throughout the country.

By the mid-1980s, Guatemaltecas were active in a wide variety of mixed-gender organizations. Responding to political and economic conditions threatening their caretaking and caregiving roles, women rallied behind organizations that offered some pragmatic relief. All of the organizations they joined subordinated gender concerns to class or ethnicity, but this did not mean that women were not conscious of gender and did not question unequal gender positions. Their participation in social movements required new skills, initiated new tensions, and activated new desires. Thus, despite the fact that most women mobilized during this early period to meet so-called material needs, clearly the boundary between practical and strategic interests was not as distinct as some interpretive frameworks have previously led us to believe. Even in this initial stage in collective action, women questioned the patriarchal definition of citizenship and gender roles. They challenged the cultural foundation of both state and civil society: the patriarchy. CPR activist Paula Carmelita adroitly demonstrates the lived relationship between the practical and the strategic:

> We've suffered, but we've also learned to solve our problems. And something we women have learned to do is stand up for our rights and be proud. It's something new and it is a little hard to do. Before women felt that because we couldn't read or write, we were only good for the kitchen, to take care of the children and all that. But now in the Communities in Resistance, we've seen a change in ourselves. Now many

women are literacy workers, health promotion workers or catechists. Some young women who didn't want to be health workers or teachers, they wanted to work with a machete, so they went to work with the men.[43]

Segments of the international community strengthened these incipient moves by Guatemaltecas to place gender on the agenda. Beginning with the 1975 United Nations World Conference on Women, held in Mexico, the Guatemalan government was slowly pulled into a series of international and regional conferences convened to discuss and recommend reforms on the condition of women. In 1981, at the urging of the Comisión Interamericana de Mujeres (Inter-American Women's Commission) and the Labor ministers of Central America, the Guatemalan government formed the Oficina Nacional de la Mujer (National Women's Office; ONAM) as the state watchdog on women's issues. Although ONAM's powers and financial resources remained minuscule, the decision by the authoritarian regime to establish such an agency at all signals the growth of domestic and international pressure on the government to bureaucratically do something about women. It is also important to keep in mind that while the state might try to define and impose certain forms upon civil society, what different constituencies do with these structures "is a different matter."[44] As we will see in Chapter 3, Guatemaltecas have tried, with only moderate success, to utilize ONAM and other state agencies for their own purposes to reform the state from within.

EXPANSION: NGOIZATION AND INSTITUTIONALIZATION OF THE MOVEMENT

In 1986, impelled by the deterioration of the economy, the expansion of civil discontent, and pressure from the international community, the military returned the government to civilian rule, although the civil war continued. The new civilian government quickly adopted an economic restructuring project.[45] The transition to a neoliberal democracy at once offered new opportunities for civil society but also presented a variety of different constraints.[46] For Guatemalan women, particularly, democratic and neoliberal reforms opened political spaces for the formation of a variety of women's groups and for the expansion of the gender debate. Within this process, however, movement organizations were also forced to reassess their goals, tactics, and strategies of collective action. So, while the women's movement expanded, it also became more professionalized, institutionalized, and NGOized. These trends helped women achieve institutional acceptability, legislative reforms, and monies for development projects targeted toward women, but they also worked to limit movement options and, at least partially, to exclude some Guatemaltecas.

Thus the election of civilian Vinicio Cerezo Arévalo to the presidency in 1986 clearly marked a watershed in the women's movement in Guatemala. After 1986, women's groups focusing specifically on women's issues proliferated. Many formed as nongovernmental organizations and sought support from international nongovernmental networks to partner projects to provide services to women. Some dedicated themselves to strategic (feminist) concerns, while others gendered larger class or ethnic concerns (popular feminists). Whether feminist or popular feminist in orientation, the organizations differed substantially in structure and objectives from earlier ones that women had participated in in the late 1970s and early 1980s.

Some organizations formed after 1986 defined themselves as feminist, but many others did not. Class, ethnicity, and geographical location generally differentiated those who adopted the feminist label from those who did not. Self-defined feminist organizations were most often founded by middle- and upper-class mestiza women in urban areas, whereas nondefined women's groups were more likely to be led by indigenous rural women. Many of the feminist leaders had participated in various ways in the popular movement of the previous decade, had been introduced to feminism in the university or during their time in exile during the repressive years, and had begun to question the lack of a gendered focus to the popular movement. Nonfeminist leaders had also participated in the popular movement during previous decades, but most lacked a firm foundation in feminist studies or political activities. Though dissatisfied with the treatment of gender by social movements, they refused to separate gender from class and ethnicity, choosing rather to engender their analyses of class and ethnicity. For these reasons, Lynn Stephen has referred to these groups as popular feminists; while rejecting identification as feminist, the groups nevertheless start from a gender analysis to explain their socioeconomic and political realities.

The Agrupación de Mujeres Tierra Viva (Living Earth Women's Group; known as Tierra Viva) and the Grupo Guatemalteco de Mujeres (Guatemalan Women's Group; GGM), two of the first self-identified feminist organizations in Guatemala—both formed in 1988 after the Latin American Feminist Encuentro in Taxco, Mexico—are cases in point. These two nongovernmental organizations, Tierra Viva and GGM, grew out of informal discussions about gender among politically active Guatemalan mestiza women exiled in Mexico and those living in Guatemala City. Tierra Viva focused on information gathering and dissemination and today runs a documentation center; holds conferences on women's health, education, and violence against women; and publishes books and literature on issues of concern to Guatemalan women.[47] The GGM, on the other hand, opened a women's center to provide social-welfare, psychological, and legal services to Guatemaltecas. Beginning in 1994, the group decided to focus solely on domestic violence and eventually opened a women's shelter in the capital city for victims of domestic violence.[48]

Although Tierra Viva and GGM at first relied on financing provided by their members, more recently they have been successful in securing international funding. In contrast to the mixed-gender movements of the previous decade, neither Tierra Viva nor GGM has received assistance from the Catholic Church. In fact, both see the church as an impediment rather than an aid in accomplishing their goals. GGM leader Giovanna Lemus, for instance, noted bitterly that GGM was forced to return a nine-year-old girl to her father who had sexually abused her after the church intervened and requested that the government order the return.[49] By the late 1980s, therefore, the church had begun to reassert the conservative construction of gender norms by refusing support for feminist groupings.[50]

Some of the feminist organizations that formed after 1986 were initially linked directly to mixed-gender popular sectors. In many cases, the women formed committees or support groups with the help and encouragement of male colleagues in the popular movements. Some of the strategic interests of the women's groups, however, ultimately came into conflict with those of the male-dominated popular movements. This led some women's groups to split from their paternal organizations. For example, in 1986, the union confederation, Unión Sindical de Trabajadores de Guatemala (Labor Union of Guatemalan Workers; UNSITRAGUA), formed a women's committee called the Grupo Femenino Pro-Mejoramiento de la Familia (Women's Group for Family Improvement; GRUFEPROMEFAM) that was composed of the wives of union leaders. The union's male leadership envisioned the committee as a support base for the struggles of the male-dominated union. The committee, however, had different goals: they conducted a study of women in industrial plants; examined the origins of sexual discrimination in plants; provided "capacity training"[51] to women workers; and helped unionize women *maquila* workers. In due course, UNSITRAGUA presented an ultimatum to the committee: "Do as we want or you won't get funding."[52]

Instead of complying, the committee split from the union and formed an independent organization dedicated to women workers. After gaining its autonomy, GRUFEPROMEFAM obtained financial assistance from a religious organization in the United States and began to provide capacity training and support services to female workers while helping them to unionize.[53]

Although most of the explicitly feminist organizations had urban bases, many of the nonfeminist women's organizations that proliferated after 1986 were rural based. These latter organizations might not have considered themselves to be "feminist," but they remained critically aware of gender inequities and made gender a focal point of their struggles. For example, the Coordinadora Nacional de Viudas de Guatemala (National Coordination of Guatemalan Widows; CONAVIGUA), formed in 1988 by indigenous women in the highland province of Quiché, rallied around the motto "For the dignity and unity of women, (we are) present in the struggle of the people." CONAVIGUA was one of the first organizations to link democracy with ethnic, class, *and* gender rights. In the process, it struggled to reconceptualize the definition of citizenship based on gender and ethnic justice maintaining a close relationship with the popular and indigenous movements:

> For women to participate, for our opinions to be taken seriously, for our dignity and rights as women to be respected. How is that accomplished? By participating in our social, cultural and religious actions, and in larger marches and demonstrations called by USAP (Unidad de Acción Sindical), we show that women must also participate.[54]

CONAVIGUA thus organized campaigns against forced recruitment and civil patrols, demanded the excavation of clandestine cemeteries, provided literacy training and health care to indigenous rural women, and called for the reclassification of rapes perpetrated during the civil war as crimes against humanity. Unlike urban feminist groups, CONAVIGUA, with its popular gendered approach, retained fairly close relations with and obtained support from the Catholic Church and the Christian Base Communities.[55] Eventually, it also sought and received funding from the international nongovernmental support network.

Women formed many other feminist and nonfeminist organizations in the post-1986 years, and each was usually formed by a small group of women united by class, ethnicity, or geographic region to provide services to other Guatemalan women who were often, but not always, from a different class, ethnicity, or geographical place. Most of the organizations rejected the confrontational politics of the earlier period and replaced them with strategy or policy politics. They lobbied the state for legislative and policy changes and encouraged women to participate in the political process,[56] but mostly they provided needed services to women—running a domestic violence shelter, providing legal services, forming women's cooperatives, providing health care, doing literacy and capacity training, to name some.

While the opening of political spaces during the early years of democratization encouraged a move away from protest politics toward strategic politics, the service-provision focus of many organizations was also bolstered by the international community's interest in economic restructuring and the subsequent growth of international nongovernmental support network funding.[57] As the neoliberal state withdrew from public servicing, NGOs stepped in to provide some of the basic necessities for citizens. Funds from the international nongovernmental support network were essential to the successful implementation of these projects. But international funding agencies were largely insistent on short-term projects that resulted in a tangible product or whose success could be measured by the accomplishment of a set task, such as helping women in a town buy a corn grinder, running a literacy training project in a village, printing educational brochures about health care, and similar service projects. Most women's groups were quite aware of the possible negatives of dependence on international funding sources, but they viewed the funding as essential. With this in mind, Guatemalteca activists contended that they carefully picked out the NGOs whose goals best coalesced with their own or ones they believed would be the least intrusive, or they tried to reduce dependency by courting several aid groups at once.[58] This, of course, was not always possible, and groups often accepted financing that came with conditions about project form, staffing, or tactics.

International funding was especially important to the fledgling women's movement in the transition years after 1986 because, despite taking steps toward democratization, the state provided little or no financial assistance and was often hostile to women organizing. It continued to underfinance ONAM and failed to pass legislative reforms considered important by women's groups. By the mid-1990s, however, the neoliberalizing state had begun to depend on women's groups to provide services it was no longer offering. Thus, though the state did not increase financial support to women's agencies and groups, it did become less antagonistic to them as it sent victims of domestic abuse to the GGM shelter, relied on CONAVIGUA to offer literacy training to indigenous women, and expected rural organizations to implement development projects. In addition, as the international community began to more enthusiastically embrace gender concerns, the Guatemalan state became more dependent on ONAM and other state-related agencies to project the state's supposed pro-women orientation to possible donors and supporters worldwide.[59]

Democratization led women's groups to reconsider their relationship with the state and to question whether to begin to work with and within the state for gendered reforms. Some—viewed as "institutionalists" by more radical feminists—ultimately decided to take the risk of joining the state to achieve perceived common objectives. One group of women, for instance, formed the Proyecto Mujer y Reformas Jurídicas (Women's Project and Judicial Reforms) associated with ONAM but independently financed by monies from Holland and Spain. The Proyecto's objective was to promote legal reforms that would improve conditions for Guatemalan women. Staffed by lawyers, the office proposed the creation of the Instituto Nacional de la Mujer (National Women's Institute; INAM)— essentially upgrading ONAM from an "Office" to an "Institute," with a corresponding increase in power and autonomy—and proposed legislative reforms on topics that included education, labor, the civil code, and the penal code.[60] Working within the state structure necessitated a new level of professionalization; class and political contacts and technological and academic training became crucial to organizational success.

In contrast to institutionalist groups like the Proyecto, other women's organizations continued to maintain their distance from the state. Like GGM, they focused on ad hoc service projects of women helping women. And though they rarely worked directly with the state, they did find it necessary to establish cordial relations with government bureaucrats and international development agencies in order to better implement their project goals. As with institutionalists, then, professional qualifications and class networks became important for ad hoc service NGOs as well. The need for higher qualifications for both institutionalists and ad hoc service providers tended to shift power within the women's movement to urban, educated mestizas who had the technical skills and personal contacts to obtain necessary funding and bureaucratic concessions.

By 1994, the women's movement had grown in number of participants, but it still consisted of many small separate organizations, each with its own goals and involved in its individual projects. Women's groups came together to coordinate special events—such as activities accompanying the November 25 International Day Against Violence Against Women— but then went their separate ways. In other words, there was an absence of a long-term sustainable relationship between the various sectors of the women's movement. The resulting factionalism definitely weakened the movement: the government and international funding agencies could deal separately with each women's organization and sometimes pit the interests of one against those of another; groups duplicated each other's work; and organizations with substantially the same objectives competed for resources and acknowledgment.

The creation of the Sector de Mujeres (Women's Sector) in 1994, in the context of the peace accords, marked another turning point for the movement, helping it to become a bit more cohesive. At the same time, it indirectly and inadvertently encouraged the further institutionalization of the women's movement. The Sector de Mujeres was the first attempt by Guatemalan women from diverse socioeconomic, ethnic, and political sectors to come together and search for common ground as women. Representatives from thirty organizations—including Tierra Viva, GGM, GRUFE-PROMEFAM, CUC, Convergencia Cívico Política de Mujeres (Women's Civic Political Convergence; CCPM), and CONAVIGUA—and eight individuals with no organizational affiliation participated in the Sector. The Sector initially represented well the diversity of Guatemalan society: indigenous women, mestizas, middle class, working class, religious, academic, feminists and nonfeminists. In fact, one of its proclaimed goals was "the search for a consensus of multisectoral groups with a respect for diversity."[61]

The Sector de Mujeres evolved from the peace negotiations between the government and the URNG and the demand from civil society that it be given a formal role in the process. Although civil society representatives were kept from sitting at the negotiating table, a compromise was ultimately reached that created the Asamblea de la Sociedad Civil (Assembly of Civil Society; ASC). The ASC was composed of representatives from almost all sectors of civil society, including youth, the indigenous population, refugees, peasants, and the working class. The Sector de Mujeres represented women in the ASC. Thus, as the state-URNG negotiations advanced, the Sector de Mujeres made suggestions to the ASC on each topic to be discussed by government and URNG representatives. The ASC then debated and presented compromise proposals to the formal negotiators. The state and the URNG took these recommendations under review during their discussions, and some of the recommendations made it into the final peace accords. This structure required compromise at every step—in the Sector de Mujeres, in the larger ASC, and finally in the peace negotiations between the state and the URNG.

Initially both left- and right-wing political factions—inside and outside the ASC—questioned the necessity of including a separate women's
voice in the peace negotiations. Both viewed the women's movement to
some degree as a foreign import; the right questioned the relevancy of
the movement to "Guatemalan culture," and militants argued that gender issues might divide the left at a critical historical moment. However,
women who joined the Sector contended that

> the Guatemalan state has always been characterized by its homogeneity,
> centralization, class orientation, militarism, patriarchy, repression and
> ethnocentrism, whose fundamental element has been violence. This
> characterization of the state is expressed in the patriarchal culture that
> excludes women from an early age from the educational system, orien-
> tating them to menial jobs, or simply to ignorance and being locked up
> in the home.[62]

This participation of the Sector de Mujeres in the ASC and the negotiation of the peace accords increased the national visibility of the women's
movement, strengthened the movement's internal organization, and provided the organizational structure to help the movement develop a multicultural, multiclassed gender analysis based on rights. It also eventually
convinced many women of the need to work with and within the state for
change.

The work of the Sector de Mujeres put gender identity politics on
the map for many in Guatemala for the first time and secured for gender a place in the final peace accords signed in December 1996. The accord documents called for gender equality in the receipt of land, credit,
and development assistance; the elimination of discrimination against indigenous women; support for gender equality in the home; equal rights
for working women; gender equity in education; and opportunities for
women in the armed forces. The accords called for the creation of the Foro
Nacional de la Mujer (National Women's Forum; Foro) to help "translate the accords into a platform of action that would include and make
viable the completion of the compromises reached by the parties who had
signed the accords."[63] Even though the accords were vague, purposefully
left open to varied interpretations, and had failed to outline implementation procedures, many Guatemalteca activists interpreted the specific
inclusion of women as a first step toward institutional change. Consequently, they were buoyed toward working to form the Foro as an effective second step.

Participation in the peace accords process convinced many women of the political validity and feasibility of working with and within state agencies for gender reform; after all, they had succeeded in making a difference in the outcome of the accords and reasoned that future successes using similar strategies were more than plausible. They thus entered the negotiation phase of Foro with a sense of purpose but were quickly and sharply reminded of the wiliness of the state and patriarchy's grip. From 1996 to 1999, the (Alvaro) Arzú government, which had ties to Opus Dei, the conservative right-wing faction of the Catholic Church, used delay tactics, bureaucratic politics, and intimidation to try to ensure that the Foro did not "get out of control" and succeed in addressing "feminist concerns such as reproductive choice and birth control."[64] The administration was aided in this endeavor by the vague directives set by the peace accords regarding the formation and structure of the Foro.

The peace accords directed that the Foro be formed during the ninety days following 15 January 1997, but they did not specify how or by whom the Foro was to be created or what structure it was to take. Women's organizations, loosely united as the Organized Expressions of Women in Civil Society, immediately began to put together a proposal for the formation of the Foro. In March, the government, wanting to take the task out of the hands of civil society, appointed ONAM to oversee the creation of the Foro. ONAM and the women's movement worked well together and moved quickly toward an accord. Unhappy with their agreement, however, the Arzú government abruptly gave the Secretaría de Paz (Secretariat of Peace; SEPAZ) — the state agency charged with implementing the peace accords and led by Raquel Zelaya, also with ties to Opus Dei — the task of negotiating the formation of the Foro. The government then appointed party bureaucrat Aracely Conde de Paiz as the Coordinator of the Foro. Conde had no ties to the women's movement or to other popular movements, and the appointment was met with universal consternation from women's groups.

After another month of bitter debate, ONAM and Organized Expressions of Women in Society were able to obtain some concessions from Conde and SEPAZ. First, Conde's position would be changed from Coordinator of the Foro to the more temporary position of Coordinator of the Installation of the Foro. In addition, a ten-member Coordinating Commission composed of government and civil society representatives under the direction of Conde was set up to oversee the creation of the Foro.[65] Despite these concessions, women's groups still complained that the government "unilaterally selected" the representatives to the commission and that feminists were not represented at all.[66] After much wrangling, the Foro was inaugurated on 13 November 1997. By 1999, it consisted of local, regional, and national units and had a membership of some 25,000 women who crossed traditional lines of race, ethnicity, language, and geographical location. The Foro was charged with overseeing the implementation of the peace accords in relation to women's issues. Though it was initially slated to be dismantled in 2000, along with other temporary organizations formed to implement the peace accords, its life span has been prolonged by yearly extensions.

There is much disagreement about whether the Foro has helped or hindered the women's movement. Some, like Valerie McNabb, maintain that the Foro was essential to "strengthening and 'consolidating peace and fostering democracy' " by providing political spaces for and civic education to indigenous women.[67] The Foro has held training seminars around the country to teach women about their legal rights and democratic participation. It has encouraged women to get involved in public policymaking, run for office, and work for institutional changes. Foro detractors, while acknowledging its many accomplishments, are often troubled by the organization's institutional focus, the numerous times the organization has been outmaneuvered by government policymakers, the lack of adequate funding for its programs at all levels, and the organization's conservative reading of gender discourses. The debates around the making of state gender policy in 1999 and the adoption of the policy document, *Promoción y desarrollo de las mujeres guatemaltecas: Plan de equidad de oportunidades 1999–2001* (*Promotion and Development of Guatemalan Women: Equal Opportunities Plan, 1999–2001*), demonstrate some of these concerns.

The idea for the *Plan* originated with a 1995 recommendation by UNICEF that every Latin American government design a formal public policy on women. The Secretaría de Obras Sociales de la Esposa del Presidente (First Lady's Secretariat for Social Works; SOSEP) was chosen over ONAM to oversee the formation of the policy in Guatemala.[68] To that end, SOSEP put together a Consejo Consultivo (Consulting Council) composed of representatives from twenty-two state institutions and civil society organizations, and in 1997 the Consejo presented public policy recommendations for review to the Secretaría de Planificación y Programación de la Presidencia (Secretariat of Planning and Programming for the Presidency; SEGEPLAN), the state planning board.[69] At the same time that the Consejo was formulating its proposals, however, the URNG and the government were negotiating peace accords that would create another bureaucracy—in addition to SEPAZ, the Foro, and the Defensoría de la Mujer Indígena (Defender of Indigenous Women)—that was also concerned with state policy toward women. After the Foro was formed, it collected data and information from women around the country and ultimately presented policy proposals to the government asking that they be included in the state's final public policy on women. The government charged SEGEPLAN with formulating the final policy document. Neither the Foro nor the Consejo—nor, for that matter, any civil society representatives—were consulted during this final process, although SOSEP and SEPAZ were given minimal voices.[70] Although the final policy document incorporates some of the Foro's recommendations, it ignores many of them. For instance, whereas the Foro proposals emphasized the need to end discrimination in the workplace, the final document skirts the issue and merely supports equal access to employment. On land ownership, the Foro recommended policies to curb gender-biased land tenure arrangements, but the final SEGEPLAN document just discussed the need to distribute technical assistance and credit on a more equal basis. While Foro policy suggestions on education stressed the need for alternative teaching methods, social and cultural sensitivity, and the participation of women in national and local administration, the final document focused on the need to educate women to bring them into the workplace in new ways. On the other hand, the final document called for policies that would encourage women's participation in the political system, a subject not addressed by the Foro proposals. It also emphatically demanded state action against gendered violence, a topic only mentioned in passing by the Foro.

Whether one interprets these results as a victory or failure for the Foro, the process helped to reveal a growing split within the women's movement between institutionalists and ad hoc project activists. Drawing upon their experiences in the post–peace accords bureaucracy, women's groups came to two different conclusions. Many interpreted their experiences in the shaping of the peace accords and the post-accord agencies in a more or less positive way. They maintained that for the first time "a space has been gained" for women, which must be taken and molded to their advantage.[71] These institutionalists sought to organize women around the public policy of rights and thus lobbied for the creation of state agencies and legislation that would protect the rights of Guatemaltecas and encourage women to participate in all areas of politics. Over the next several years they fought relentlessly for institutional changes: the use of gender quotas in political parties, legislation that outlaws violence and discrimination against women, more autonomy for ONAM, and ways to increase female electoral participation.

Other groups, however, came to the opposite conclusion after working in the post-accords bureaucracies: that the time, energy, and money they were using to try to change institutional behavior was failing to achieve the desired ends. They argued that despite the dedication of individual women and groups, the state was still succeeding in subordinating, co-opting, and repressing gender reforms and the political participation of women. While supportive of public policy changes, these project activists reinvigorated their focus on civil society by supporting ad hoc service projects, generally funded by international NGOs, to aid women — literacy and leadership training, women's health and reproductive rights programs, and economic subsistence projects.[72] Some of these activists also attacked patriarchal ideological structures. Women's groups, for example, started radio programs to discuss women's issues; one small group of feminists started the first feminist newspaper, laCuerda; and lesbians formed Mujer-es Somos (We Are Women), which provided a physical space for lesbians to gather but also advocated cultural change through the visibility of same-sex desire. By the beginning of the twenty-first century, the Guatemalan women's movement was gaining strength in numbers, but it remained divided over strategies and goals.

SUMMARY COMMENTS

Prior to 1986, the state and social movement activists were on a collision course; women's and other social movements were demanding a radical revamping of state and society, starting with a redefinition of citizen and citizenship. By 2000, many women's organizations were either working with or within the state for institutional reform or implementing ad hoc service projects that in the past would have been considered government responsibilities. Most women's groups had become nongovernmental organizations with standard bureaucratic structures supported by international funding. The transition from revolutionary/protest politics to lobbying, policymaking, and ad hoc service shifted not just movement tactics and structures but also power, both within women's organizations and between the movement and the rest of civil society. The new demands on organizations privileged professional women who had not only technical and management skills but also the personal class, ethnic, and urban elite connections to work the state and funding bureaucracies. They needed to write funding proposals, assemble and manage the staff to implement projects, get government permits, lobby state agencies for support, write legislative reform bills, and provide statistical proof of the success of their programs to benefactors. In the class and ethnically polarized

Guatemalan society, these skills privileged mestiza upper- and middle-class urban women. In contrast, the clients serviced by women's organizations were increasingly poor, rural, and, often, indigenous. The rising division between the provider and client roles thus replicated the stark class and ethnic factionalism of the larger society. Though there were many exceptions to this trend, the NGOization, professionalization, and institutionalization of the movement after 1986 favored division rather than unity within the women's movement and between Guatemaltecas.

> *Los acuerdos de paz reconocen la necesidad de que la mujer*
> *participe ampliamente en la construcción de la democracia en*
> *Guatemala y ejerza a plenitud sus derechos civiles y políticos.*
> *Para lograrlo es necesario superar la discriminación.*[1]
>
> — MINUGUA

Debates over the meaning and the construction of *democracy, citizenship*, and *rights* have dominated the political modernization project of the postauthoritarian era in Guatemala. Most, though not all, state and civil society political actors agree on the need to build democratic institutions and reframe the relationship between the state and civil society, but they disagree about the breadth, direction, and timing of democratic reforms. Women's organizations have maintained that democracy cannot be achieved without the full participation of women. Consequently, they have tried to position themselves to influence the form and content of institutional reforms. The results have been mixed; in some cases women have succeeded in challenging the patriarchal institutional structures, and in others they have submitted to what Cynthia Enloe refers to as the patriarchy's "global malleability."[2]

By the end of the twentieth century, feminist scholars had begun to analyze the complexity of women's participation in transitional democracies. In Guatemala and many other Latin American countries, women have struggled for rights on a different trajectory than that expressed by the classic model of T. H. Marshall,[3] who argued that political rights (political participation and power) and then social rights (economic welfare and security) would *follow* the attainment of civil rights (individual freedom). But in Guatemala, and in much of Latin America, women initially mobilized during the authoritarian regimes to demand a combination of first social and then civil rights. Only at the end of the civil war, as political space offered by civilian governments opened opportunities, did women begin to acquire political rights.[4] Whether or not this trajectory difference has led to or helps explain varied postauthoritarian political developments is still unclear, but democratization is unmistakably affecting Guatemalan men and women in ways that differ, both between the two sexes and from their respective counterparts in the North. It is thus imperative to look more deeply into the potentials and limitations of democratization for women in transitional postwar societies. To that end, one must explore changing definitions of citizenship, the manner in which citizenship continues to be gendered, and the ways in which female citizens are being categorized. Democratic transition by definition requires discussions regarding the rights of citizens. Within the neoliberal context of Guatemala's transition, however, an emphasis on the obligations and self-reliance of citizens is shifting rhetoric and policies away from what the state can do for its citizens to what citizens can do for the state. In fact, the trend noted by Carole Pateman in the North about defining citizenship by the contribution of employment, is increasingly being adapted to nations in the South like Guatemala as policymakers ask how women can best contribute to national economic development.[5] Meanwhile, pressured by women's groups and the international community, the democratizing state in Guatemala has assumed a public agenda of gender equity and has started to address gender issues institutionally.[6] As shown in the previous chapter, women's groups are thus moving from opposition to the state to participation within the state structure, struggling to turn the latter into a site of engagement where women can help to dismantle masculinized privilege. Although many students of and activists in postwar transition societies contend that gender equity is at least partially linked to the degree of participation of women in the transition, others stress that the "status of a local woman, any woman, in the postwar setting" is also crucial. It is thus important to examine not only female participation but whether or not transition decision makers continue to define women in terms of their prewar roles or what they were doing during the war — as heroic mothers, victims of sexual assault, or enemies of the state. As Cynthia Enloe maintains:

> Some categories are useful in the making of policies and the nurturing of cultures that foster genuine democratization and demilitarization. But narrow, war-referenced categories into which many women are placed by journalists and decision-makers — even categories that seem to valorize some women — can become the basis for crafting patriarchal and militarized public policies.[7]

This chapter examines some of these issues in relationship to the women's movement in postwar Guatemala. Is the discursive and legislative legitimacy of talking and making laws about women and their rights as citizens helping women to dismantle masculinized privilege in Guatemala? How are new institutions and legal constructs categorizing Guatemaltecas? How are concepts of femininity being mobilized to meet the needs of changing political institutions? In what ways are the presumptions of citizenship based on self-reliance and contribution shaping, altering, and limiting the objectives, strategies, and achievements of the women's movement? What benefits, problems, and changes have arisen for the movement in working with a state that has adopted an external agenda that, on the surface, addresses some of the objectives of the women's movement?

The peace accords of 1996 committed the Guatemalan government to legislative and institutional reforms. While it has failed to fully accomplish these goals, pressured by women, the international community, and the necessities of neoliberal economics, the state began to rethink public policy on and social categorizations of women. Ultimately, the government passed three laws between 1996 and 2003 that created the legislation, discourse, and institutional structures for a more gender-sensitive state agenda, but it simultaneously also confirmed patriarchal notions about Guatemaltecas. To better understand this dilemma, we need to examine changing masculinized and feminized meanings in postwar Guatemala.[8]

REDEFINING WOMEN: FROM MOTHERS (SOME HEROIC, SOME NOT) TO WORKERS

Defining "women" for the purposes of the law has been difficult and often contentious in postwar Guatemala. Should the law separate indigenous and mestiza women? Should it treat all Guatemaltecas the same, or should it recognize their differences? How can equity and diversity be simultaneously legalized? Guatemalan women have been grappling with these questions as they have struggled to engender the law.

Guatemalan law is hierarchical, with the constitution at the apex. In 1985, as the military government prepared to step down, a new constitution was promulgated that remains in effect today. The 1985 Constitution defines gender biologically and bases equality on difference that necessitates special treatment for women. While granting men and women equal opportunities and responsibilities (Article 4), the constitution exempts women from the death penalty (Article 18); maintains that "maternity is protected by the State" (Article 52); protects human life from conception (Article 3); protects the social, economic, and legal role of the family; commits the state to fight against alcoholism, drug addiction, and "other causes of the disintegration of the family" (Article 56); protects female workers from doing certain work (not specified) during pregnancy; guarantees pregnancy leave of thirty days before and forty-five days after birth with pay; and grants new mothers the right to breast-feed a baby on the job twice daily (Article 102).

Liberal feminists would contend that such special treatment actually perpetuates gender discrimination.[9] Accepting the contention of liberal political theory and political institutions that "the liberal ideal of equality is itself neutral vis-à-vis gender," they maintain that the "appropriate response to the inequality between the sexes is for women to pursue the ideal of neutrality more rigorously: to hold liberalism accountable to its own professed ideals."[10] Difference theorists, on the other hand, argue that liberalism may appear neutral, but in reality it is andocentric, or male defined, and thus law and citizenship must be reconstituted drawing "maternal thinking" into the political arena.[11]

In 1985, the government's Oficina Nacional de la Mujer (National Women's Office; ONAM), formed in 1981 as the state watchdog on women's issues, came into this debate on the side of inclusive difference and succeeded in getting articles on the family, marriage, and reproduction included in the constitution. As a consequence of ONAM's intervention, the constitution bases difference and special treatment of "women" as a universal group on their reproductive role. This approach, however, fails to recognize varied gender perspectives of the diverse Guatemalan population.

The peace accords addressed diversity in a more consistent manner. Prodded by the Sector de Mujeres, negotiators ultimately recognized women not only as wives and mothers or in their wartime roles as widows, displaced persons, and victims of sexual violence, but also as indigenous persons, heads of families, peasants, workers, and citizens. The accords urged the government to eliminate gender discrimination in accessing land, housing, credit, and other productive and technological resources,[12] acknowledging that "the contribution, inadequately valued, of women in all economic and social spheres, particularly their community work, . . . coincides with the need to strengthen the participation of women in economic and social development on the basis of equality."[13] The peace accords initiated the propensity, expanded by future legislation, to shift the primary definition of women as mothers and wives to one that included their economic contributions to national and community development.

Even as the accords questioned some dominant gender categories, they upheld others. The most striking are the subtle differences they make between indigenous and mestiza women. Despite the surface attempts by negotiators to address the concerns of indigenous women and recognize ethnic diversity, the wording of certain agreements can be interpreted as the disempowering of indigenous women in discursive and material ways. This is most apparent in a section of the "Acuerdo sobre Identidad y Derechos de los Pueblos Indígenas" (Agreement on the Identity and Rights of Indigenous Communities) labeled "Rights of Indigenous Women." Though this accord rightly deserves recognition for its advancement of multiculturalism, it continues to reflect long-standing patriarchal and racist sentiments toward indigenous women. For example, before acknowledging the double discrimination of indigenous women on the basis of ethnicity and gender,[14] it "recognizes the special vulnerability and defenselessness of the indigenous woman."[15] While both the state and the law can be criticized for not "protecting" the rights of indigenous women, to label them as "vulnerable" and "defenseless" disavows indigenous women as empowered subjects. Categorized as victims, they are erroneously perceived as passive and immobile.

This victimization is continued in the next paragraph, despite the fact that it recommends the passage of legislation that would criminalize sexual assault. Indigenous women's groups fought for the accords to denounce gendered violence perpetrated by the military against indigenous women during the war. The recommendation for criminalization is thus generally interpreted as a victory for women's groups in general and for indigenous women in particular. Still, the wording of the article is ambiguous, weakening its potential use by indigenous (and other) women to eradicate sexual abuse. The article states that the government should "promote legislation that classifies sexual assault as a criminal offense, considering as an aggravating factor in determining the penalty for sexual offenses the fact that the offense was committed against an indigenous woman."[16] Consequently, the agreement recommends legislation that would criminalize all sexual assaults against everyone—male/female, mestizo/indigenous, young/old. Indigenous women are thus elevated to the status of all other citizens; sexual offenses against them are sexual offenses. At the same time, the agreement stipulates that the penalty for a sexual offense against an indigenous woman might be greater than in other cases. No explanation (historical or otherwise) is given for this, however, thus skirting any analysis of ethnic polarization, discrimination, or blame for the gendered violence of the war. The ambiguity of the recommendation not only fails to provide indigenous women with a soundly based argument for redress but seems to divide mestiza and indigenous women with its unexplained and vague ranking of sexual abuses.

Some of these problems—most notably defining "woman" and specifying the role of difference—persisted into the three laws passed in 1996, 1999, and 2001 to address some of the concerns of women outlined in the peace accords. The *Ley para prevenir, sancionar y erradicar la violencia intrafamiliar* (Law to Prevent, Sanction, and Eradicate Violence within the Family) was approved in 1996; the *Ley de dignificación y promoción integral de la mujer* (Law for the Dignification and Integral Promotion of Women), in 1999; and the *Ley de desarrollo social* (Law of Social Development), in 2001. The first two laws partially follow previous international agreements already ratified by the government, and all three forced a reconstruction of gender categories. Women inside and outside the government were active in forming and passing all three laws in their effort to further engender the law. Unfortunately, the laws, though appropriating the language of gender equity, do not completely dismantle traditional constructions of women, femininity, and masculinity. In addition, though the laws have helped to mainstream women and institutionalize the women's movement, they have also contributed to limiting the debate about gender.

ENGENDERING DOMESTIC VIOLENCE

The Women's Defense Program was created in 1992 within the Human Rights Ombudsman's office, and it was this office, supported by various women's NGOs and the congressional Commission on Women, Children, and the Family, that shepherded the *Ley para prevenir, sancionar y erradicar la violencia intrafamiliar* through the Guatemalan Congress to its approval in 1996. Some women preferred a law that would eradicate all forms of violence against women, but they could not garner enough support within Congress, and thus the *Ley para prevenir sancionar y erradicar la violencia intrafamiliar* came into being.

The law subscribes in some aspects to a similarly named agreement, the *Convención interamericana para prevenir, sancionar y erradicar la violencia contra la mujer,* signed in Brazil in 1994. There are major differences between the two, however—a fact that is partially obvious from their divergent titles. Whereas the *Convención interamericana* condemned *all* violence against women, the Guatemalan law passed in 1996 only addresses intrafamily violence, that is, domestic violence against any member—male or female—in the family. Even though Guatemalteca rights activists lobbied hard for a law more similar to the *Convención interamericana* agreement, the Guatemalan Congress, claiming a desire to keep the law neutral,[17] penned a final bill that replaced violence against women with intrafamily violence. In doing so, Congress subtly attempted to turn attention away from any discussion of gender politics and power inequities.

The new law tried to stabilize patriarchal constructions of gender. Thus, according to the law, women (mothers, wives, and daughters) were as guilty of family violence as men (fathers, husbands, and sons). Although women were rarely specifically mentioned, when they were, the law extended the tendency found in the 1985 Constitution of inappropriately linking women with minors, the elderly, and the handicapped (Article 2). Finally, the law did not set out to punish the nongendered abusers but to "regulate the application of means of protection" and to "offer protection" to abused family members. These methods of protection entailed actions such as taking the abuser from the home, ordering him/her to enter therapy, confiscating his/her guns, and temporarily taking away custody of minor children. The law is thus confined to monitoring an abusive situation after it has already happened and does not extend to preventing the abuse or punishing the perpetrator. In its entirety, the law does much to uphold the culture of violence against women rather than attack it at its patriarchal core.

If this were the end of the story, we would have a typical state-versus-women dichotomy. However, as Georgina Waylen has noted, states are themselves gendered; they not only help to construct gender and gender relations but are also shaped by activities of women and the women's movement.[18] Waylen maintains that "if the nature of the state or the relationship between the state and gender relations is not fixed and immutable, battles can be fought in the arena of the state. The state is therefore 'an uneven and fractured terrain with dangers as well as resources for the women's movement.'"[19] Accordingly, while the *Ley para prevenir, sancionar y erradicar la violencia intrafamiliar* sought to restrict major changes to gender relations, the women's movement used the law to force the government and society to make some adjustments.

Soon after the passage of the law, women's groups formed the Red de la No Violencia contra las Mujeres (Network for No Violence against Women) to coordinate their lobbying and practical work around the issue of violence. Unlike the law, the Red concerned itself with all violence against women—private and public—and explained violence as embedded in unequal relations of power.[20] The Red organized conferences, marches, and protests around the November 25 International Day of No Violence against Women, but it also pressured the government to implement the *Ley para prevenir, sancionar, y erradicar la violencia intrafamiliar* and to pass new legislation that would criminalize all violence against women. To accomplish these goals, the Red mounted a multipronged attack that included institutional, protest, and interpretive strategies. The Red and its members thus publicized the law, assisted women in making denouncements of abuse to the proper agencies, created a standard form to make the denunciation process easier and more efficient, collected statistics on domestic violence, and lobbied for the formation of the Coordinadora Nacional para la Prevención de la Violencia Intrafamiliar y en contra de la Mujer (National Coordinator for the Prevention of Violence within the Family and against Women; CONAPREVI) and for the passage of another law—ultimately named the *Ley de dignificación y promoción integral de la mujer*—that would, among other things, regulate against public and private gendered violence.

After the passage of the domestic violence law, Red members not only helped to publicize the law but also gave it a popular feminist interpretation. A pamphlet published and distributed by four indigenous women's groups—Majawil Q'ij, Ukux Ulew, Defensoría de la Mujer Maya, and the Asociación de Mujeres Nuevo Amanecer (Women's New Dawn Association)—intersperses a popularized version of the law with illustrations of indigenous women as victims of violence but also as individuals empowered before indigenous and mestizo patriarchies. The pamphlet states, for example, that Article 1 of the law defines intrafamily violence as

> the damage and suffering that any member of the family causes to another family member. That damage can be in the form of blows, pulls, abuses, insults, breaking things (furniture, dishes, etc.), sexual injuries or abuse. This violence is almost always committed by the husband or ex-husband against the wife, although it can also be done by other family members (*suegros, cuñados, hermanos*).[21]

It then goes on to discuss how women can use the law to protect themselves from domestic violence. This and other similar interpretations by Red members differ significantly from those of government agencies. The original law does not privilege women, nor does it denounce men as the aggressors. A brochure distributed by the congressional Comisión de la

Mujer, el Menor y la Familia, for instance, stresses the intrafamilial focus of the law and fails to gender domestic violence.

The illustrations in the two brochures highlight their varied interpretations—violence as gendered or not. In the brochure distributed by Majawil Q'ij et al., violence is gendered; illustrations depict victims as indigenous women and children, and abusers as men—primarily indigenous men. In the congressional pamphlet, almost no victims are shown. In one drawing a mestizo boy is being grabbed by a mestizo man, and in another a mestiza woman and her child are speaking with a man behind a desk. In the women's brochure, indigenous women are shown as being empowered by the law as they take on positions of authority to help other indigenous women combat violence. In the government's version, although faces of smiling indigenous women appear on a front cover collage, the only other picture of an indigenous woman is one in which a woman and her two children are standing a bit behind a happy mestizo family. Not one of the other six illustrations portrays indigenous individuals at all. In fact, indigenous males are completely absent from the entire brochure.[22]

Thus, through interpretation, Guatemaltecas came to take at least partial ownership of the *Ley para prevenir, sancionar y erradicar la violencia intrafamiliar*. As another part of their strategy, the groups in the Red lobbied the government for more forceful legislation to combat violence against women. They focused on two legislative reforms: (1) a bill to create an administrative body to oversee the implementation of the *Ley para prevenir, sancionar y erradicar la violencia intrafamiliar*, and (2) the passage of the *Ley de dignificación y promoción integral de la mujer*, which was being promoted by many women's groups within and outside the Red to put national legislation in line with international laws already ratified by the Guatemalan government. In a clear victory for the women's movement, both laws were eventually passed. A closer examination of the laws, however, reveals the potentiality that they may post numerous roadblocks to gender equality.

As its first effort at public advocacy, the Red promoted the passage of a bill to establish the administrative arm that would implement the *Ley para prevenir, sancionar y erradicar la violencia intrafamiliar*. In November 2000, they succeeded, after several failed attempts, in getting Congress to approve an amendment to the original law, creating the Coordinadora Nacional para la Prevención de la Violencia Intrafamiliar y en contra de la Mujer (CONAPREVI). CONAPREVI was charged with ensuring the effective execution of the *Ley para prevenir, sancionar y erradicar la violencia intrafamiliar* by coordinating the work of all government agencies involved with domestic violence (law enforcement, judicial, and others) and violence against women. For Red members, it was key that CONAPREVI (re)gender the law by highlighting violence against women. Whereas the original law had limited discourse to nongendered domestic violence, CONAPREVI reopened the dialogue once again to understanding violence in relation to gendered power relations. At the same time, CONAPREVI altered the Red and its focus from a loose activist and lobbying network to an institutional participant.

CONAPREVI is a public agency, but it is composed of representatives from both the public sector (four members) and the Red (three members). Although the formation of CONAPREVI is viewed by most in the women's movement as a victory for the Red, institutionalization has been accompanied by difficulties. The agency, a dependency of the presidency, is not sufficiently independent, nor has it received the financial resources to accomplish the desired goals of Red members. Consequently, CONAPREVI has been forced to seek funding from the international community, which has come with the common dilemmas associated with outside financing.

PROMOTING THE DIGNITY AND "COMPLETENESS" OF WOMEN

Following the lead of the Red de la No Violencia contra las Mujeres, some members from the Red and other organizations formed a loose coalition, the Coordinator of Women's Legal Actions (Coordinadora de Acciones Legales de las Mujeres; COALM)[23] to advance the passage of another women's law, the *Ley de dignificación y promoción integral de la mujer*. After three years of COALM's lobbying congressional delegates, organizing activities with the press, and hosting public forums in which the proposal was presented, the law was finally approved in 1999.[24] The *Ley de dignificación y promoción integral de la mujer* is far reaching in denouncing economic, political, and social discrimination against women. It also condemns violence against women in all its private and public forms. While the law recognizes the multicultural and multilingual nature of Guatemalan society, it clearly positions the stability of the nation in the family and thus guarantees the rights of women in relationship to the family—as wife and mother but also as a breadwinner—and requires that the family, community, and state take the necessary steps to protect women in these roles. The law consequently calls for increasing the education of women; giving women technical training; providing family planning education to women; granting women access to land; improving women's access to credit; and helping to guarantee women's participation in politics. The state is charged with ensuring that families, communities, and the larger society provide these opportunities to women. The law thus moves the public into the private realm by requiring that the state guarantee that women be allowed by their families to work, that mothers and fathers act responsibly and as equal partners in the home, that families send girls as well as boys to school, and that men be punished for committing violence against women. In actuality, then, the law calls for no less than the reordering of gender and gender relations.

Although the law goes further than any other law in Guatemalan history in denouncing gender discrimination and inequality, it nonetheless presents gender constructs that could be both empowering and disempowering to Guatemaltecas. Plainly, the law provides women with a legal basis from which to demand equality or at least equal opportunities from the state. But the concept of "equality" is limited by the law's positioning of women in relationship to their families. The roles that women were expected to play in the Guatemalan family one hundred years ago clearly are not the same as those of today. For example, until 1998, the Guatemalan Civil Code gave husbands the authority to deny their wives the right to work outside the home, and until 1999, the Code contended that women could only work outside the home if it did not prejudice the interests and care of their children.[25] The new law, in contrast, orders the government and families to assist women to work outside the home.

Still, by continuing to define women *only* as part of a heterosexual family, as the law does, it limits discussion of women's rights to those issues considered by the dominant society at any given moment to be acceptable concerns for heterosexual family women. The concerns of unmarried or childless women, women in same-sex partnerships, and any other women who do not define themselves by their family roles cannot be addressed. Although the *Ley de dignificación y promoción integral de la mujer* defines a "modern" version of the family, which secures some new rights for Guatemaltecas, by continuing to use the nuclear family as a starting point for gender construction, it narrows the conversation about and possibilities for femininity and masculinity constructs.

In addition, the law positions the interests of women and their families firmly within a technicalized understanding of development. Accordingly, to achieve "dignificación y promoción integral" (dignity and fulfillment,) women must become clients of and helpmates to the state's modernization project. The law thus calls upon the state to guarantee women equal access to education, technical training, credit, employment securities, and better reproductive services. In exchange, women will become productive (neo)citizens.[26]

Despite limitations, both the *Ley para prevenir, sancionar y erradicar la violencia intrafamiliar* and the *Ley de dignificación y promoción integral de la mujer* took concrete steps toward laying the legal basis from which to challenge some important aspects of the existing patriarchy in Guatemala. Both laws validated the expansion of women's roles in national political and economic development by stipulating that women have more power over their own bodies and the resources needed for their fuller participation. The *Ley de desarrollo social* followed this legislative trend, completing the legal trilogy that created the foundation of neocitizenship for Guatemalan women.

A WOMAN'S PLACE IS IN DEVELOPMENT

Passed by Congress in September 2001 over the heavy protest of the Catholic Church,[27] the *Ley de desarrollo social* creates the legal procedures and structures by which the state can both "promote, plan, coordinate, execute, and evaluate" national development and bring women into its national economic development project. Many of the issues expressed in the previous two laws are revisited in the *Ley de desarrollo social* but with a developmental emphasis. Again, the law designates the family as the basic unit of society; however, the definition of the family is extended beyond just married couples to include nonmarried male/female partners and single-parent households. The definition not only fits more closely with the reality of contemporary Guatemalan family structure,[28] but also widens somewhat the possibilities of conceptualizing gender and gender relations.[29] With the well-being of the family at its center, the law calls for responsible maternity and paternity, which includes providing children with the necessary material goods for their "desarrollo integral" (complete development)[30] but also practicing family planning, ending gendered violence, and ensuring that children are educated, including receiving sex education. Meanwhile, the state is called upon to improve educational and health care services to help families meet their obligations.

Women's interest groups supported the basic tenets of the *Ley de desarrollo social* in the heated societal debate that occurred prior to its final approval.[31] Even as the Catholic Church and other conservative forces decried the bill's support for family planning and sex education, women's groups supported it for highlighting many of the issues the movement had long fought for—reproductive health care, familial respect for women, acknowledgment of women's part in economic development, and equal access to education. For state modernizers, on the other hand, the bill was important as a means of furthering development through population control and integrating women into the labor force in new ways.

After the passage of the law, women's groups once again utilized interpretive and advocacy tactics to shape the contours of the law. As with the *Ley para prevenir, sancionar y erradicar la violencia intrafamiliar*, women popularized and interpreted the new law for their constituencies, molding it to fit their needs whenever possible. For instance, a feminist news source stressed the empowering aspects of the law to its readers, saying that the law signaled that

> every person has the right to make responsible and mindful decisions about her family and reproductive life. To do this, she has to receive prompt and complete information. Reproductive health and family planning programs should lead the distribution of information. The Minister of Health should elaborate, inform, and diffuse information about the use of contraceptives.[32]

Other organizations embraced the law as a way to increase women's political participation in the planning and execution of state development policies. The *Ley de desarrollo social* charges the Consejos de Desarrollo Urbano y Rural (Councils on Urban and Rural Development), a decentralized administrative arm of the government, with organizing and coordinating national development policy. The Consejos were first introduced by the 1985 Constitution[33] but were revamped and codified to support the *Ley de desarrollo social* in 2002. Today, the councils are composed of representatives from both state and civil society and are organized at five levels (national, regional, departmental, municipal, and community). Women are assured of representation at all levels, albeit in slightly different ways. The national Consejo, for example, is directed by the president, with representatives from various government agencies; the coordinators of the regional Consejos; and representatives from indigenous groups, cooperatives, large and small manufacturers, workers, peasants, development NGOs, and women's organizations. The community-level Consejo, in contrast, is composed of all members of the community it represents— men and women—who elect a mayor and a coordinating committee to preside over it. In an attempt to decentralize development policymaking, each level of Consejo collects information on the needs and priorities of their constituents, reports this to the Consejo body above it, and helps to implement approved development projects. Final plan decisions and financial distribution, however, rest with the national body and ultimately with the president.

Women's groups targeted the Consejos as key to bringing rural and urban women into the development process and institutionalizing their political participation. Consequently, they have widely publicized the importance of these bodies and have organized capacity training sessions to encourage women to take an active role in the Consejos. Their WID-like tactic,[34] however, is not without its critics, who question whether women's concerns and demands will succeed in reinterpreting development or fall victim to being reinterpreted by development.

The Consejos are still too young to make pronouncements of their success or failure, but their structure does allude to areas of potential concern for the women's movement. Despite its purported goal of decentralization, the Consejo structure remains fairly hierarchical: the president holds final decision-making and purse-string powers, and lower bodies have little autonomy to act without support from above. In fact, some critics see the Consejos as a way for the central government to recapture powers lost to development NGOs during the 1980s and 1990s. They contend that the Consejo administration redirects both development decision making and financing away from independent NGOs back to the government bureaucracy, albeit with input from civil society. Although many activists hope that the structure will prove inclusionary and democratic, some fear that it may ultimately favor the voices of the development technician and professional. While the Consejos provide the structure by which people can participate, their technical duties—collecting data, prioritizing development projects, writing proposals, putting together budgets—may silence many.[35] In fact, the law ensures the payment of a technical team for each Consejo, a policy meant to assist but one that could lead to the subordination of nontechnical to technical approaches and solutions. Finally, some have worried about the executive branch's commitment to the process. They hope that what happened on the inaugural day of the national Consejo—when President Portillo failed to arrive and the Vice President had to step in and preside over the meeting—is not a sign of the executive's disregard for the opinions of civil society.[36]

The post–peace accord years thus marked a convergence of forces encouraging the mainstreaming of gender, at least partly as a means of bringing women into the workforce in new ways. As a consequence, and with the participation of the women's movement, laws were passed, policies were created, and institutions were formed—all purporting to support gender equity. As these institutions proliferated, the women's movement lobbied for a more autonomous and powerful state agency to coordinate and execute government gender policies. Women's groups, however, could not agree on the structure, powers, and focus of the agency. Should ONAM be restructured and given more autonomy and powers? Should the Foro take charge of coordinating public policy on women? As debate continued, conflicting bills were presented to Congress, indigenous and mestiza women's groups differed over a decentralized versus a centralized structure, and existing government agencies struggled to ensure their position in any new configuration.[37] In 2000, however, the Portillo government halted the debate by creating the Secretaría Presidencial de la Mujer (Presidential Women's Secretariat; SEPREM).

INSTITUTIONAL REPRESENTATION: SECRETARÍA PRESIDENCIAL DE LA MUJER

SEPREM was charged with coordinating "public policies for the development of women" and functioning as the "government focal point for the maintenance of a permanent dialogue with the rest of civil society."[38] Women's groups played almost no role in the creation of SEPREM, and most, at least initially, were deeply dissatisfied with it. They believed that despite its ministerial powers, SEPREM was still a dependency of the president. Thus, when they were called upon to suggest names for the first director, only one women's group, the Sector de Mujeres, did so. All others boycotted the process. Still, many were pleasantly surprised when the president approved the Sector's choice and appointed Dr. Lili Caravantes as the Secretaria Presidencial. Although disunity—within both the women's movement and the state government—allowed the executive more maneuverability to structure the form and content of SEPREM, the choice of Caravantes as the first Secretaria satisfied a wide range of feminist and state factions and tended to bring feminists back on board. Caravantes possessed many of the political and class connections regarded by the state as critical for anyone leading the state's gender mainstreaming effort, yet she also had close ties with national women's groups. Caravantes had worked for eleven years with the Pan-American Health Organization before taking over the Secretaría and was well connected with both the international funding community and Guatemalteca activist groups. Her international connections would be essential for the health of SEPREM, because though the state would provide most of the funds to sustain SEPREM's payroll, the agency would have to solicit funding from the international community to finance most projects.[39]

In many ways Caravantes proved to be an able administrator of SEPREM, although some women maintained that her original support of the women's movement was ultimately overshadowed by her role as a bureaucrat.[40] She created an organization with a staff of fifty-two, helped negotiate the government's Política Nacional de Promoción y Desarrollo de las Mujeres y Plan de Equidad de Oportunidades for the 2001–2006 period, and maneuvered bureaucratic conflicts concerning oversight powers between SEPREM, the Foro, and ONAM. As head of SEPREM, Caravantes took part in the Consejo Nacional de Desarrollo and CONAPREVI, represented the government at international conferences on women, and worked to both engender and implement government policies. In 2003, for example, SEPREM was involved in the government's reproductive health, antipoverty, and citizenship campaigns.

Many of these roles have benefited both the state and women in Guatemala. SEPREM helps to channel international funding to public programs for women, provides a positive space for dialogue between the women's movement and the government, and pushes for legislative and administrative gendering. Even so, there are structural concerns that weaken SEPREM's ability to be an inside advocate for Guatemalan women. Like other government agencies in Guatemala, SEPREM at times falls victim to the volatility of Guatemalan politics and to a structure long dominated by clientelism, violence, and corruption.[41] While Caravantes worked hard to keep the agency free of corruption, increasing its appeal to international funders, she was not always so successful in keeping it above the fray of bureaucratic and party politics. In addition, SEPREM's reliance on international funding has limited its ability to plan, prioritize, and execute long-term projects. International donors are most interested in contributing to the implementation of short-term projects that have clear, measurable results, but objectives like the reconstruction of gender imagery, one of the areas in which Caravantes thought the agency should be doing more,[42] are difficult to concretize into such units. In addition, SEPREM and other state agencies lack staff with a firm theoretical foundation in gender studies. Caravantes acknowledged that although everyone talks about mainstreaming gender, many do not really understand what gender is all about, leading to public policies that are inadequate at best. Moreover, though the Secretaria urged women to stop portraying themselves as victims — "somos pobres, somos indígenas, somos campesinas" (we are poor, we are indigenous, we are peasants)[43]—some women contend, with good reason, that institutionalization of women's concerns has not always empowered women, thus perpetuating a feeling of victimization on the part of some.[44]

The new structures are working to free women from some constraints, but they are also categorizing women in ways that continue to limit their participation in all aspects of civil society. Trends toward professionalization and clientelization of the women's movement noted by Sonia Alvarez and Veronica Shields in other Latin American countries are, in fact, being replicated in postwar Guatemala. Institutionalization is giving a voice to a few professional Guatemaltecas—those who have the education and class connections to write funding proposals and legislative bills, lobby for public policy reforms, and direct and work in institutional offices. But in a system marked by extreme socioeconomic and political inequality, institutionalization also encourages a patron-client relationship between professional women within the institutions and nonprofessional women (poor and/or indigenous) outside the institutions. No matter how hard they try, mestiza professionals in Guatemala City have a difficult time representing the interests of indigenous poor women from a variety of ethnic and economic backgrounds in the countryside. Victimization is sometimes an understandable consequence of this situation.

CONCLUSIONS

The signing of the peace accords signaled the beginning of state attempts to reconceptualize Guatemaltecas. At the same time, the postwar period offered women a chance to participate in restructuring the political system. Consequently, new laws were passed that dealt with violence, reproductive health, and gender discrimination. In addition, a number of new government agencies—often with the participation of the women's movement—promoted the engendering of public policy. Even as the state continues to base women's identity in the family in the postwar period, the definition and needs of the family and state are changing and thus so too are gender positions. In postwar Guatemala, women are still represented as wives, mothers, and daughters legislatively and by public policy. But they have also become recognized heads of households, farmers, workers, and community builders. Increasingly, women are seen as a critical part of the labor force needed to build a healthy immediate family and a prosperous nation-family, so the state has begun to take steps to help reconstruct gender relations in ways that will allow women to more effectively perform their development responsibilities. Supporters of the Guatemalan women's movement have labored diligently with and within the state to try to structure institutional reforms to meet their needs as much as possible. Despite this, they have not always been able to accomplish their goals.

Although the institutional patriarchy is gradually being altered in Guatemala, it is not being eradicated. One last legislative example distinctly demonstrates this. In August 2000, women's groups succeeded in sending to Congress for discussion a bill that would regulate the work of domestic workers, 70 percent of whom are indigenous women. The bill proposes the improvement of working hours and conditions for these workers but actually reinforces the traditional patriarchy and stereotypes of indigenous women. It lists thirteen obligations and prohibitions for domestic workers, including "observe good habits/customs" (*observar buenas costumbres*); be honest, responsible, and diligent in carrying out the instructions of one's employer; respect the employer and his/her family, friends, and neighbors who visit the home; do not allow unknown people to enter the employer's home without the employer's permission; and do not leave work during working hours without the permission of the employer (Articles 17 and 18). Another list is provided for employers, which includes prompt payment of salaries, respect for time off, permission for visits from family members to domestic workers during time off.[45] If passed, the law would guarantee domestic workers a modicum of protection as laborers, but it would also continue to support the unequal power relations between indigenous women and the masculinized mestizo family.

Almost no one, and especially not Guatemalteca activists, would ever argue that legal reforms will miraculously translate into gender equality. Activists contend that the women's movement must fight for equity on multiple fronts—legislative, institutional, material, and cultural. Democratization has in some ways constricted political spaces for the women's struggle by funneling women and their demands into institutional spaces that control debate. The state's focus on state modernization has put women in a difficult position. If they do not participate in the democratization process, state reform might take place without their input. If they do work with the state, women's groups and agendas might be reshaped, constrained, or co-opted.

Still, though many groups like those discussed in this chapter work with and within the state for institutional change, others have turned to identity politics both to strengthen civil society and to prod it into reexamining its notions of gender and sexuality. Identity politics, criticized by many in northern academic circles as limiting, has become one focus around which indigenous and lesbian women have built autonomous organizations in Guatemala to address discrimination based on gender, sexuality, and culture. Identity movements, however, have become reliant on the international community not only for funding but, at times, for defining identity discourse also, which leads to an interesting conundrum. What is the relationship between identity and the local and the global? How are local political identities forged within the expanding global social movement network? How are global discourses altered and manipulated by local movements? Chapter 4 examines the lesbian movement's attempts to organize around identity to destabilize male privilege within homosexual and heterosexual communities and cultures.

Chapter 4

T IS FOR *Tortillera?* SEXUAL MINORITIES AND IDENTITY POLITICS

*What's the connection? I asked, between a tortillera and a
lesbian? Something to do with the sound, they said, the
kneading of masa and palms rubbing together, the clapping of
tongues, the intersection of good taste and the golden touch.*[1]

— ALICIA GASPAR DE ALBA, "DESCARADA/NO SHAME:
A[BRIDGED] POLITICS OF LOCATION"

In 1991–1992, a group of gay male friends in Guatemala City, fright-
ened and saddened by the increase in HIV/AIDS deaths of homosexuals
in Guatemala, began to meet informally to educate themselves about the
disease. They arranged for a Costa Rican expert on HIV/AIDS to visit
Guatemala to give a talk. That event was a success, so they continued
to hold meetings and discussions. After several months, however, they
decided that there was more than just a need to discuss and educate
about HIV/AIDS; there was also a need to establish a safe and secure
space where homosexuals could meet away from the culture of violence
and homophobia of Guatemalan society. In 1993 they founded the not-
for-profit Organización de Apoyo a una Sexualidad Integral frente al
SIDA (Organization to Support an Integral Sexuality in the Face of AIDS;
OASIS).

Even though OASIS primarily serves the lesbian/gay/bisexual/trans-
gender (LGBT) populations, it has remained closeted, maintaining fairly
separate public and private agendas. Overtly, OASIS engages in HIV/
AIDS prevention in Guatemala, but privately it mainly works with, and
seeks to provide a safe haven for, sexual minorities in Guatemala City.[2]
OASIS' president, Jorge López Sologaistoa, defends the dual agenda by
noting that the only way the organization could have obtained the legal
standing to operate was to conceal the sexual orientation of the organization's focus.[3] By 1996, OASIS was able to provide institutional space
and support for the formation of the first lesbian collective in Guatemala,

which was ambiguously named Mujer-es Somos. In 1999, members of Mujer-es Somos started Lesberadas (Collective of Liberated Lesbians), later changed to Lesbiradas (Collective of Liberated Lesbians and Bisexuals) to accommodate bisexual members. In June 2000, OASIS and Mujer-es Somos supported the country's first Gay Pride March, organized by the newly formed Grupo Promotor del Colectivo Gay-Lésbico de Guatemala (Group for the Advancement of the Gay and Lesbian Community in Guatemala) and led by Fernando Bances, one of the founders of OASIS who had begun to criticize OASIS' closetedness.[4] In 2002, Lesbiradas became the first "out" association in Guatemala to receive legal status as a not-for-profit organization, and it moved into its own office space in downtown Guatemala City.

It is tempting to simply interpret these developments as a sign of the successful internationalization of gay politics and the viability of identity politics as a liberating strategy. LGBT populations in Guatemala *are* slowly organizing, making themselves visible, and demanding rights. These developments are very real, but this chapter explores the complicated intersection of the global with the local in Guatemala. It examines the varied and sometimes contradictory ways in which the junction of global and local is shaping gay—specifically, lesbian—and identity politics in Guatemala.

INTERNATIONALIZING GAY POLITICS

Through the 1970s and 1980s, gay identity politics in the United States was at least partially established on what John D'Emilio suggested were the "myths" of the invisibility and the eternity of homosexuality.[5] Using these myths to construct and politicize a lesbian identity in the United States, lesbians built a movement in two distinct stages: the first was preoccupied with establishing a local identity, and the second, with more global questions and connections.[6] As a result, the U.S. lesbian movement moved from an emphasis on "fixing lesbians as a stable identity group" to constructing a lesbian culture founded on resistance to gender and sexual norms. Clearly, "coming out," rewriting histories, and "in-your-face" politics were logical politicizing and mobilizing tools of the movement's founding constructs.

Some argue, however, that over time the global gay movement has erroneously come "to perceive these U.S. gay liberation tactics of political mobilization and community cohesion as 'reliable' indicators of sexual orientation around the world. These myths, when coupled with biological determinism, reinforced the notion that the origins of sexual identities are fixed"[7] within and across time and space. Heather McClure, Rosalind Morris, Dennis Altman, and others have forcibly argued for a context-based understanding of sexuality. Morris notes: "We know that the apparatus of power is different in every society and that the discourses of sex and gender differ from context to context. Yet a considerable body of critical theory persists in a mode of historical analysis—the emphatically linear genealogy—that derives from the West's specific experience of modernity."[8] To move away from linear genealogy, there is a need, as Altman contends, for a "political economy of homosexuality, one which recognizes the interrelationships of political, economic, and cultural structures."[9] As a consequence, consistency "as an overriding principle [of identity politics] would be replaced by a high regard for context."[10]

Following this nonlinear genealogical model, the study of sexuality in Guatemala needs to be made within the diverse socioeconomic and political contexts that shape the lives of sexual minorities. We must examine the ways in which global discourses and strategies of identity politics intersect with and possibly affect this local context. How have local definitions of femininity and masculinity shaped gay politics in Guatemala? How has the acceptance (or not) of global labels such as *homosexualidad, gay, lesbiana,* and *bisexual* expanded or limited understanding and practice of sexuality in Guatemala? Are processes of democratization, neoliberalization, and globalization significantly altering the conditions under which Guatemalan sexual minorities define themselves and relate to the larger Guatemalan community? Is the homosexual/heterosexual division that came to dominate the United States in the mid to late twentieth century being replicated in Guatemala? Are these developments privileging some actors and marginalizing others? Can modernity be linked to the creation of a universal gay identity?[11] Do Guatemalan sexual minorities link behavior and identity or do they separate the two?

To begin to answer some of these questions, this chapter focuses on the incipient mobilization and politicization of a small group of lesbian and bisexual women. The form, goals, and strategies of the organization, I argue, are firmly rooted within the context of Guatemala's political economy. An understanding of the Guatemalan gay *ambiente* (environment) must therefore incorporate traditional conceptions of sexuality, the impact of the civil war and democratization, and the rise and development of local and global gender- and human rights–focused discourses and organizations. At the same time, however, the rising importance of the three "izations"—institutionalization, NGOization, and globalization—on the debates within, and the organization of, sexual minorities in Guatemala must be considered.

MEXICO: LEFTISTS, FEMINISTS, HOMOSEXUALS, AND LESBIANS

Lesbian groups already had some years of organizational experience in many Latin American countries by the time the Mujer-es Somos collective, the first such organization in Guatemala, formed in 1996. Timing and context have been critical in shaping the movement in Guatemala. This can best be shown through a regional comparative perspective, contrasting the experiences of neighboring Mexican lesbians with those in Guatemala.

Norma Mogrovejo argues that the Mexican lesbian movement is rooted in three interconnected movements: those of left-wing youths, feminists, and gays.[12] Many early lesbian activists were deeply involved in the anticapitalist and pro-justice student movement of the 1960s and 1970s. From that base, they joined both the second wave of feminist organizing and the male-dominated gay movement in the 1970s. By the late 1970s, however, many had become vocal against what they perceived to be the exclusionary agendas of both feminists and gays. Attempts by lesbians, for example, to push the feminist movement to address the needs of sexual minorities were often rebuffed—though feminist leaders privately expressed support for individual lesbians, they argued that it would be politically unwise to include lesbian demands in the larger feminist agenda. As Yan María Castro remembered to Mogrovejo:

> When I said to them [women in the Coalition of Women] "I'm a lesbian," they found it very shocking. At first they said to me: "We love you very much anyway." Or they would say: "It is OK for you to be like that. We respect all women here. But maybe it is best if you do not make this known to the outside world."[13]

Using some of the same arguments previously used by leftists against the inclusion of gender issues in the class analysis, many feminist activists maintained that lesbian needs would ultimately be met by the gender-equity demands of the women's movement, and that the inclusion of lesbian-oriented concerns would irrevocably divide the women's movement at a critical time in its formation.[14]

Though many lesbians remained convinced by these arguments, some did not. Dissatisfaction led to the formation of a few small lesbian groups that aligned themselves with or worked within the male-dominated homosexual movement, thus creating a lesbian-homosexual coalition. Like Mexican feminists, male homosexual organizations had roots in the earlier left-wing student movement, and, in general, the gay movement retained a class and social justice focus. By the mid-1980s, however, the lesbian-gay alliance had started to fall apart; women accused the men of phallocentrism. Others—men and women—criticized the "toothless" nature of the coalition, and a growing number called for the depoliticization of the movement because they "just wanted to have fun."[15] At the sixth Gay Pride Parade in Mexico City in 1984, tensions between lesbian and male homosexual activists exploded when some of the male marchers arrived and "played around" with large hand-made foam phalluses.[16] According to one participant, "That bloody march was very aggressive from the moment that the boys arrived with those things; it looked like a carnival of the phallus. They arrived with those great big pricks." In response, a lesbian leader "threw a paper airplane which she had set alight at one of the pricks and it caught fire."[17]

For many women, that march was the moment when male/female difference took preference over desire, leading to a split from homosexual men. Some women returned to the feminist movement, and others set up autonomous lesbian groups closely linked to the women's movement. Despite the difficulties, heterosexual women and lesbians slowly moved closer together, united against a perceived oppressive patriarchy. Nationally and regionally, heterosexual and lesbian women began to talk with each other to build common ground. As one feminist activist in Mexico said, "We [heterosexual feminists] came to the lesbian meeting and saw lesbians in flesh and blood, talked to them, saw they were like us."[18] In due course, some began to see lesbianism not simply as an erotic-affective possibility but as a political alternative.

The Mexican lesbian movement followed a localized version of the decentering path taken by the women in Arlene Stein's U.S. study. Like their U.S. counterparts, many Mexican lesbians came out of feminist and leftist movements to construct a *lesbian* category, a *lesbian* identity, and *lesbian* institutions. Eventually, they began to use their constructed identity as lesbians to contest the "dominant sex/gender system."[19]

The politicization trajectory of Guatemalan lesbians differs in critical ways from that of their counterparts in Mexico. First, the timing and origins of the movement are different. Lesbians in Guatemala did not begin to organize until the 1990s, long after Stonewall,[20] the crisis of HIV/AIDS, and the growth of an international gay movement. Second, lesbian organizing did not grow out of student left-wing or feminist movements, but evolved at the end of a long and violent civil war that had led to the growth of a national preoccupation with human rights and citizenship inclusion. Third, many lesbians in Guatemala define lesbianism as behavior and sexual practices, not as an identity. These differences, at times, conflict with the identity-politics focus of some lesbian activists in Guatemala who are affiliated with the global gay community.[21]

LESBIAN IDENTITY OR SEXUAL BEHAVIOR:
I AM OR I DO

Dennis Altman and others argue that individuals who have same-sex relations do not necessarily identify themselves as gay, not out of "ignorance" or "fear," as some gay activists insinuate, but because they have different perspectives of and on sexuality.[22] In many cultures, sexual practices do not join neatly with sexual identities, and individuals who have same-sex sexual relations often define themselves as heterosexual, if sexual identities are marked at all. The *pasivo/activo* distinction made by some Latin American men to distinguish between heterosexual and homosexual men is an often-cited example: only *pasivo* (penetrated) men, and not *activo* (penetrating) ones, in same-sex relations consider themselves and are considered to be homosexuals. On this matter, Stephen Murray writes, "real men are indifferent to the sex of the orifice into which they thrust,"[23] making gay men only those who "act as women" in same-sex relations. Still, as Heather McClure notes, "These categories are far from stable . . . and may be less indicative of actual sexual positions or roles . . . than of the parameters or possibilities of male social identities."[24]

The origins of the *activo/pasivo* divide are contested, but Jorge López Sologaistoa of OASIS cites machismo as of key import. Quite simply, he argues that society discriminates against women and thus it—and the gay community—also discriminates against men who are perceived to be "like women" in and out of bed. To illustrate his point, he related the time he and another man were in a car kissing. When confronted by the police, the officers interrogated and insulted López Sologaistoa's more effeminate partner but said nothing to López Sologaistoa, who considers himself to be a masculine man. His partner was perceived to be "the pervert," Sologaistoa argues, because of his effeminacy.[25] Here, a perceived feminine performance marks the authenticity of homosexuality. What does this say about the relationship between performance and identity; that is, does performance determine identity or vice versa?

Increasingly, in Guatemala and in other regions of Latin America, there is a shift away from the *activo/pasivo* hierarchy within the male homosexual community. Extending López Sologaistoa's thesis, one could argue that the women's movement has not only opened up space for women but also for a dialogue on gender; as the position of women changes in society and as femininity discourses are questioned and altered, the subjective role of those perceived as effeminate homosexuals might also change.[26] However, it was clear in an interview with López Sologaistoa that awareness of global gay discourses is also influencing gay activists to encourage the dismantling of the *activo/pasivo* difference. Changing attitudes toward *activo/pasivo* will not necessarily translate into the development of a gay identity as expressed in the North, although the dismantling of the *activo/pasivo* distinctions could open the way to reworking labels, the perceptions of sexuality, and gay politics. Thus, we must keep in mind, as Steve Pile does, that "engagements in the politics of location . . . involve the definition of boundaries—but . . . they are not to be seen as fixed, impermeable, and permanent."[27]

Guatemalan lesbian activists affiliated with the global gay community are working to build a lesbian political identity using a trajectory similar to that used by groups in the United States and Mexico. In July 2000, Lesbiradas issued the first (and, to date, the only) edition of its magazine, *Identidades: Lesbianas guatemaltecas en su diversidad.* The magazine is dedicated to "recuperating our history" and "constructing a future," and the editors write, "We propose that the recuperation and the construction be a collective project."[28] Accordingly, Lesbiradas leaders Claudia Acevedo and Samantha Sams are researching and planning to write a history of "Lesbian identities in Guatemala." Lesbiradas has recently moved into its own institutional space, a house in central Guatemala City, where they host talks, conversations, workshops, and poetry readings for and with lesbians in the capital. Through the struggle toward visibility, group leaders hope not only to sensitize a homophobic dominant community but also to build a cohesive lesbian community. To this end, they occasionally plaster areas of the capital city with bold stickers proclaiming, "Basta! No more invisibility: Lesbians are everywhere," "Basta! No more exclusion: Lesbians for education free from prejudices," and "Basta! No more discrimination: Lesbians have rights."

These and other identity-building strategies of Lesbiradas are attempts to build a lesbian identity that counters the dominant Roman Catholic-based patriarchal discourses and homophobic policies toward Guatemalan sexual minorities. Still, as McClure contends, the connections between sexual minorities in Guatemala and the global gay movement may have inhibited the formation of "local" identities and thus may result in incongruity between lesbian "activists" and other more local "lesbians."[29] The relatively late timing of lesbian organizing in Guatemala, compared with that in Mexico, is significant, as is the key participation of several non-Guatemalan northerners in the Guatemalan lesbian collectives. Clearly, many Guatemalan homosexual activists are encouraged by discourses of human rights and HIV/AIDS prevention and have been attracted to the northern model. All the same, it could become a problem for movements if those discourses and strategies do not appropriately address the reality of how people in a particular location feel about and experience their sexuality,[30] which could lead to the marginalization of the life experiences of some sexual minorities and the inappropriate privileging of others.

MUJER-ES SOMOS, MUJERES FUIMOS: THE ORIGIN OF LESBIRADAS

The origin of Lesbiradas is found in the lesbian collective Mujer-es Somos. Mujer-es Somos was formed in 1996 under the auspices of OASIS, which gave the collective a space and a small amount of money to begin to "provide [lesbians] a harmonious and safe place to share their identity." The collective organized talks, educational forums, and social events designed to help create an "environment between us"[31] by providing lesbians with a place to discuss, debate, and reconcile their differing attitudes toward issues of identity. At the center of an evolving split was a conflict over the definition of lesbianism. Some saw the collective as the first step toward the politicization of a newly constructed lesbian identity, while others maintained that to be a lesbian merely signified a woman who had sex with other women. Thus to this latter group, lesbianism started and ended with sexual behavior.

These differences are clearly expressed in an early collection of interviews with collective members undertaken by Inés Rummel, a young German woman active in Mujer-es Somos. Rummel approached the interviews from a so-called Western-movement context; she assumed a two-stage progression from the creation of a "local" lesbian identity to a politicized systemic questioning focus. Many of those interviewed, however, had trouble or were uninterested in addressing issues of consistency, history, or identity. In fact, only one interviewee, the artist Guanda, responded directly to Rummel's questions about history and consistency.

Guanda claimed that in the 1960s–1970s "there were already men who dressed in feminine ways, men that made themselves up and women who acted totally masculine. One woman, for example, resembled Rock Hudson and another resembled Paul Newman because it was the Hollywood era." At the same time, Guanda labeled herself differently in different circumstances: she called herself a bisexual when she was talking about the fact that she has a daughter, and a lesbian or gay when discussing her sexual relations with women. Unlike Guanda, Mélida refused to search for the roots of her lesbianism. Like the majority interviewed, she defined lesbianism as "sex between women" and said, "I've been a lesbian since approximately the age of fifteen. I don't want to talk about the 'why'!"[32]

Rummel got similar resistance when she asked the interviewees when they "came out of the closet." Some responded vaguely about being perceived as boys when they were children. For instance, Patricia said, "We hung out in a group of five or six friends [girls] and they treated me not like a [female] friend, but a [male] friend." Others recounted childhood crushes on teachers or classmates.[33] Despite claiming to be "out," they all continue to conceal their sexual orientation from their families, coworkers, and non-gay friends. The openness, visibility, and identity politics usually connected with coming out of the closet in the North is less critical and certainly more diffuse in the Guatemalan interpretation.

It is interesting that Guanda—the one who is economically better off, has had a foreign girlfriend, and has traveled outside Guatemala—is the only one to conform to Rummel's movement trajectory. Class, in fact, remains a significant variable of identity formation within the Guatemalan lesbian community. Urban upper-class lesbians have the northern vocabulary to discuss gender and identity politics and the financial means to live fairly independent lives with their partners. At the same time, the unspoken rule "Don't ask, don't tell" shapes their lives; as one woman interviewed noted, "Everyone knows who is with whom, but no one talks about it."[34] In contrast, financial insecurity more often means that working- and lower-class urban women continue to live with parents, husbands, or other relatives. Their movement outside the home is more restricted, both by family and by finances. Still, lesbians of all classes feel constrained to use performance techniques to hide their sexual preference, dressing in "feminine" ways, having boyfriends, and/or getting married.[35]

Class differences impact not only the women's private lives but also efforts to organize based on identity. Although the upper-class lesbian may have the vocabulary of identity politics, she has been less willing to participate in lesbian organizations or projects. This may be because upper-class women have more to lose in the way of money and social standing if they question or challenge dominant social norms.[36] It may also partly be due to the fact that working-class women have a longer history of organizing out of necessity. Acevedo notes that "generally, working people see organizing as a more urgent matter, as a means of survival, while the bourgeois have other resources. What I mean is that it is easier to attract working-class lesbians to our group, activities, and public work, than those who have means, jobs, businesses."[37] At the same time, however, society is more lenient with upper-class women because of their class standing; if they are not openly critical of dominant gender norms, they will be allowed to maintain a "deviant" lifestyle behind closed doors. Consequently, for upper-class lesbians, sexual preference often takes on only secondary importance. In 1997, Heather McClure interviewed a wealthy lesbian couple who lived in a gated community in Guatemala City, concluding that "Lilian and Ana's social world seemed more constricted by the frequent kidnapping of members of wealthy families for ransom than by the actuality or anticipation of sexual-orientation-based violence."[38]

By the late 1990s, Mujer-es Somos faced a significant crisis. A number of the collective members wanted to politicize the organization, using it to confront, dismantle, and replace the homophobic and sexist culture in Guatemala. They argued that for it to do so, the organization would have to "*out*" itself and openly fight for lesbian rights. Divisions within the organization grew between those who preferred to keep a focus on the personal and those who pushed for an orientation that was "a bit more political."[39] Similar tensions also began to separate Mujer-es Somos from OASIS. The question of focus ultimately led to changes for Mujer-es Somos.

Mujer-es Somos had grown up within OASIS. Unlike in Mexico, the Guatemalan lesbian groups that have emerged have had few historical connections with feminism or left-wing politics, although some individuals in them, including some leaders, have a history of activism in popular and revolutionary movements. Instead, group political identity was discursively and organizationally based within the incipient gay community as defined by OASIS. HIV/AIDS provided OASIS with the impetus and rationale to organize, but within the context of three decades of political violence, the organization chose not to adopt an openly gay identity.[40] OASIS legally organized to work in HIV/AIDS prevention, and though it also facilitated other support services and social activities for the gay community—including computer training, a youth empowerment program, conferences on gay identity, parties, and so on—the majority of its directors continued to support a dual and half-hidden mission. Mujer-es Somos had been born and nurtured in this dual setting.

Mujer-es Somos' dissatisfaction with OASIS came from several sources in the late 1990s. First, some women became frustrated with what they perceived to be OASIS' disrespect for the concerns of lesbians. They argued that OASIS' focus on HIV/AIDS and its insistence on remaining closeted took a disproportional amount of money, staff time, and political maneuvering away from demanding and defending the human rights of all sexual minorities. On the most basic level, lesbians felt marginalized by men in the gay movement in general and within OASIS specifically. They argued that OASIS had been founded, and continued to be led, by men in support of the interests of male homosexuals and that the sexist behavior of the dominant culture permeated the organization. McClure confirmed a strong feeling of sexism/subordination of women in the organization after a visit in 1997.

> Lesbians at OASIS hold lower status than male members. I was provided a small but stark example of this when I asked a staff person (one of five at the time) if I could use a box of their cookies (which I promised to replace) for my interviews with members of Mujer-es Somos. In response, he retorted that he did not see why OASIS' cookies should be used for "their" meetings.[41]

Lesbians felt marginalized not just within OASIS but by the entire male-dominated gay *ambiente*. Often cited is the fact that Pandora's Box, the oldest gay bar in Guatemala City, initially allowed women into the establishment only if they were accompanied by a man.[42] And Acevedo notes, "In queer community spaces, most of the activities are geared to gay men. They say they are open to all, but then they ask you to contribute a condom to let you in."[43] Movement policies and strategies, lesbians argued, also disenfranchised women. Again Acevedo explains, "A few days ago, for example, a group called the Lesbian-Gay Collective declared a National Day of Lesbian and Gay Dignity without consulting anyone else. We at Lesbiradas [as the only lesbian organization] felt they had rendered us invisible."[44]

Some OASIS leaders admit to organizational cliquishness and now say that they recognize the different needs of Guatemalan lesbians. Still, they argue that lesbians always had a voice in OASIS and note that the by-laws of the organization require that the board of directors be composed of seven individuals—four from one sex and three from the other. "Sex" is self-defined, however, and thus transvestites who consider themselves "to be women" serve on the board as women. Consequently, the board could very easily be composed of the required two "sexes" but lack lesbian participation. In addition, OASIS leaders defend the closeted and less political nature of OASIS against attacks from Mujer-es Somos. They fear that an open, human rights, in-your-face political approach would heighten aggression against gays and their organizations.[45] They cite the culture of violence and the apprehension that all Guatemalans and gays live under, list the numbers of violent attacks perpetrated each year against gays, and note that the gay label is still strategically used to discredit individuals and groups.[46]

After the shooting near OASIS' office of María Conchita, a transvestite sex worker who had volunteered as an AIDS educator at OASIS, the gay community organized a public vigil to protest violence against gays. Some leaders of Mujer-es Somos pushed OASIS to build on the momentum of this public display to mobilize gays behind a demand for the human rights of sexual minorities. However, Samantha Sams, Acevedo's Canadian-born partner and colleague in Lesbiradas, observed, "Many people in the gay community, especially middle- and upper-class gay men [which McClure notes dominate OASIS], remained wary of the human rights discourse—fearing it 'smacked of subversion'—and have refused to take on an explicit role as human rights defenders of sexual minorities."[47]

The tensions within Mujer-es Somos and between the collective and OASIS intensified. By 1998, Mujer-es Somos was on its last leg, and in 1999 some of the Mujer-es Somos activists started Lesberadas, which later became Lesbiradas at the request of the bisexual members. By 2001, the tension between OASIS and Lesbiradas was so great that Lesbiradas formally split with OASIS, and as López Sologaistoa joked, "Mujer-es Somos" became "Mujeres Fuimos."[48] Lesbiradas received its legal status as a lesbian organization in 2002 and moved into its own space supported by the HIVOS, an NGO based in Holland that is one of the major supporters of OASIS and women's groups in Guatemala.[49]

The split between OASIS and Lesbiradas was rancorous, and tensions remained at the end of 2002.[50] In many ways, the conflicts resemble those between lesbian and male gay communities in Mexico and the United States. Like their northern counterparts, Lesbirada activists now argue the need for an autonomous lesbian organization fighting openly for lesbian visibility and rights. Tactically, they are trying to build alliances with other social movements around human rights and inclusionary citizenship discourses. They are thus joining the national and regional debates over the "appropriations and definitions" of the notion of citizenship that "largely constitutes the grounds of political struggle in Latin America."[51]

Until the beginning of the twenty-first century, the lesbian community had almost no history of alliance building in Guatemala. Though a few lesbians had previously participated in left-wing feminist and other organizations, they had always done so as closeted individuals. Unlike in Mexico, therefore, left-wing politics and feminism had had minimal foundational influence on lesbians in Guatemala. These movements did help to open up political spaces to conversations about gender, but lesbians did not incorporate their intellectual contributions into their own struggle. In fact, the vast majority of those interviewed by Rummel in 1995 denied that there was any relationship at all between feminism and lesbianism. Moreover, many confused feminism with feminine/femininity, as Mélida did: "For me to be a feminist is to be coquettish in every way: in dress, walk, attitude. The purpose of feminism is to get the attention of men, and I am not like that."[52] Liga added that, to her, feminism "meant to be a woman who is happy being a woman. I am fascinated by [meaning attracted to] feminine women. I don't like it if they are just like me. Feminine women have always gotten my attention because they are feminine."[53] Although these responses frustrated Rummel (she notes after Liga's comments that "I interrupted here to explain that 'feminism' is another thing from being feminine!!"),[54] they demonstrate a substantial distance between feminism and lesbianism in Guatemala.

In contrast, some Lesbirada leaders link their sense of lesbianism directly with feminism and see the connection as one of the starting points for politicizing lesbianism. Acevedo comments, "I'm not a typical example of what it is to be a lesbian in Guatemala . . . I've been politically active, openly, for some twelve years now, in Left and feminist groups."[55] In a similar fashion, another leader concludes, "I identify as a lesbian because I, as a woman, love other women, because my primary relations are with women, I give my vital energies to her, and I see my reflection in the faces of other women that also love women."[56]

Unlike in Mexico and the United States, where lesbian identity was profoundly influenced by feminism (despite the array of disagreements), in Guatemala, lesbians did not articulate their lesbianism in feminist terms or through any overt political critique, at least according to most of Rummel's interviewees. This could be due to the exclusion—self-imposed or not[57]—of lesbians from the Guatemalan women's movement. It might also allude to a form of gender norm subversion; by substituting femininity for feminism, Guatemalan lesbians may be rejecting femininity "as an organizing principle of their own sexual identities."[58]

Alliance building has not been easy for Guatemalan lesbians. Some social activists have privately been supportive of Lesbiradas, and women's groups are slowly beginning to informally discuss sexual preference and the rights of sexual minorities.[59] Many groups still contend, however, that the formal incorporation of lesbian rights into their organizational platforms would prove divisive. In addition, some maintain that Guatemala has many other more important problems that have to be dealt with first.[60] Consequently, an attempt by Lesbiradas and other gay organizations to garner support for a draft law against discrimination based on sexual orientation or identity is moving slowly. Although the draft law does not address gay marriages or immigration rights for partners within same-sex couples, it would provide the legal groundwork from which to fight some discrimination against sexual minorities. The bill calls for the reeducation of relevant government personnel, such as police and members of the public prosecutor's office, as well as reforms to education, health services, and the judicial system "to promote awareness, inclusion and respect of sexual diversity in human rights–related cases."[61]

By linking lesbian politicization to human rights discourse, activists are trying to use local and global discourses and concerns to both construct and politicize a lesbian identity. The experiences of the long civil war, together with international debates around human rights, have helped to propel rights and the notion of citizenship to the center of social movement organization in Guatemala. Lesbiradas has joined indigenous people, women, the poor, and others in Guatemala who are demanding inclusion. Encouraged by support from the international rights community, Lesbiradas is attempting to push for full citizenship for sexual minorities. It remains noteworthy that Sams and Rummel, two non-Guatemalan lesbians, are playing important roles in shaping Lesbiradas' identity and politics. The Dutch HIVOS group has provided Lesbiradas with the financial ability to separate from OASIS and establish an autonomous identity-based organization.

Nevertheless, one has to ask whether an incongruity exists between Lesbiradas' objectives and strategies and the ways in which the majority of Guatemalan lesbians experience and feel about their sexuality. In general, Guatemalan lesbians define lesbianism as behavior, not as an identity. In some ways, they are more similar to young, so-called postfeminist lesbians in the United States, who do not regard lesbianism as a feminist or political act. They, too, are taking the identity out of lesbianism. But

Guatemalan lesbians have not come to this juncture as a "third stage" after identity construction and politicization. In contrast, lesbian activists affiliated with the global gay community are trying to build a movement based on identity by assuming the trajectory used by lesbians in the North. These strategies may ultimately succeed for some, but in "succeeding," they may also marginalize the varied histories and experiences of other Guatemalan sexual minorities. At the same time, northern discourses may only partially displace historically based constructs of sexuality. Activists may talk about "coming out," lesbianism, bisexuality, and the like, but they may not always be able to control the meanings of those discourses within the Guatemalan context.

Global and local interests intersect in the next chapter around the relationship between globalization and gender as it relates to women in the workforce. In looking at the expansion and operation of the maquiladora industry in Guatemala, it becomes clear that the industry not only depends on traditional gender norms to control the female-dominated workforces, but it also sets the stage for a rethinking of those same gender regimes. The balance between change and tradition is a delicate one for all involved: female/male, employer/employee, industry/state, and national/international community. While some patterns can be determined, there is nothing predetermined about the results of the interactions in which various participants are involved.

*We are women and we've organized . . .
what have you men done?* [1]

—MERCEDES BARRIOS, GUATEMALAN FACTORY WORKER

Although not usually recognized as such by mainstream literature, gender is the lynchpin of globalization: to achieve globalization's expansionist goals, the restructuring of capital accumulation requires the reevaluation of social reproduction and gender relations. Whereas industrialization of the 1950s–1960s lured Guatemalan men to the factories, recent developments are pulling women, often for the first time, into the *maquilas* and the formal economy.[2] This female proletarianization is contributing to the rethinking of gender constructions in Guatemala at both private and public levels. The traditional male-dominated household must adjust to the increased buying power of its female participants and to their absence from the home during the long workday, and institutions—including unions, private sector entrepreneurs, and the state—must contend with the presence of and need for women in the modernization process.

Although economic restructuring necessitates reconceptualizing gender constructs, it also relies, at least at this stage, on discrimination based on the capacity to reproduce. *Maquilas* and other such industries are dependent on cheap labor, weak or nonexistent unions, and favorable taxation and capital repatriation regulations. In their attempts to ensure a cheap, malleable labor force, shop managers replicate patriarchal structures on the factory floors, which are numerically dominated by Guatemalan women. Still, the changing economy and gender roles are leading to the growth and strengthening of activism based on popular feminism in the factories. Guatemaltecas are organizing and participating in unions; joining activist networks; and rethinking gender roles at home, in the streets, and on the shop floor. Thus one dilemma of globalization is its need to rethink gender and at the same time use patriarchal structures to control labor.

NESTING IN THE "LAND OF ETERNAL SPRING":
THE HISTORY OF THE *Maquilas* IN GUATEMALA

In Guatemala, the *maquila* industry, dominated by apparel manufacturing, has expanded rapidly since the mid-1980s. In 1984, there were only six *maquilas* operating in Guatemala, employing fewer than two thousand workers.[3] By 2003, according to the Comisión de la Industria de Vestuario y Textiles de Guatemala (Guatemala Apparel and Textile Industry Commission; VESTEX)—the industry's association within the larger private sector group, the Gremial de Exportadores de Productos No Tradicionales (Nontraditional Products Exporters Association; GEXPRONT)—there were more than 228 apparel factories, 36 textile mills, and 260 firms that supplied accessories or other services to the industry. The apparel *maquilas* alone employed some 93,450 workers in 2002, approximately 80 percent of which were women.[4] Apparel exports have become an important source of foreign exchange, increasing from $6.4 million in 1983 to $407 million in 1999 to over $1.6 billion in 2001.

The use of the term *maquila* in Guatemala is said to originate in the word *makila*, used during colonial times to refer to the portion of flour that the miller kept for himself for grinding a farmer's corn.[5] Today, the term refers to a factory contracted or subcontracted by transnational corporations to perform the last stages of a production process—the final assembly and packaging of products for export. Transnational corporations supply *maquilas* with the preassembled materials, such as cloth and electronic components, and *maquilas* then employ workers to assemble the materials into finished or semifinished products, which are then exported back to the transnational corporation.[6]

The profitability of the factory depends on a cheap, flexible labor force; weak or unenforced labor laws; low capital investment; and simple and nonintrusive state export regulations. If these conditions change, *maquilas* are prone to quickly pack up and relocate to more favorable environs, gaining them the nickname in Guatemala of "swallow industries," signifying their swift migratory abilities.

The expansion of the *maquilas* in Guatemala that burgeoned in the mid-1980s was the result of a combination of global economic factors and the concerted efforts of the governments of Guatemala, the United States, and Korea. Beginning in the early 1970s, transnational corporations faced a severe crisis of profitability in their northern factories. As profit rates fell, corporations tried to convince workers to accept givebacks, but they met with heavy resistance from unionized workers. Companies that could feasibly make the shift south began to do so in search of more favorable environs. Despite the existence of low wages, weak unions, and few government restrictions in Guatemala, transnational corporations initially bypassed it for other hosts, including the Dominican Republic, Costa Rica, and Mexico, among others. During this period, both the Guatemalan and the U.S. governments tried wooing transnational capital to Guatemala with little success.[7] The Guatemalan state passed three laws that presented monetary incentives to companies establishing themselves in Guatemala, and the U.S. Agency for International Development (USAID) spent millions of dollars fostering the production of nontraditional agricultural and *maquila* products for export.[8]

Despite these incentives, however, the growth of *maquilas* in Guatemala during the 1970s and early 1980s was minuscule. Explanations for this slow start have included corporate fear of the civil war's political violence; concern over the possibility of expropriation if the URNG did succeed in taking power; the absence of an independent national entrepreneurial sector in Guatemala; the earlier failure to control unionization efforts by a New York City–based company, Transcontinentales S.A.; and the absence of sufficient numbers of qualified workers (often said to be based on racist comments about rural indigenous workers). Probably all except the last reason have some validity. In any case, after the election of civilian president Vinicio Cerezo Arévalo in 1986, the *maquila* industry began growing by leaps and bounds, with the United States becoming Guatemala's most important textile and apparel trading partner. The value of apparel exports from Guatemala to the United States increased from $22.4 million in 1986, to $50.6 million in 1987, to $142.7 million in 1989, to $203.3 million in 1990, to $349.6 million in 1991.[9] By 2001, Guatemalan apparel exports to the United States had risen to a value of $1.6 billion.[10]

This growth can only be understood in the context of the concerted effort by several governments—Guatemalan, Korean, and U.S.—to increase apparel and textile production in Guatemala. In 1983, the Reagan administration initiated a series of free trade policies with Caribbean and Central American nations, which were modified over the next twenty-some years. The 1983 Caribbean Basin Economic Recovery Act (CBERA) gave the U.S. president the power to exempt from tariffs certain goods imported from specified beneficiary countries of the Caribbean Basin for up to twelve years. Although apparel and textiles were not directly eligible for CBERA tariff preferences, the Special Access Program allowed production-sharing tariff relief through bilateral agreement between CBERA members and the U.S. government.[11] In October 2000, President Clinton named Guatemala a beneficiary of the new Caribbean Basin Trade Partnership Act (CBTPA) passed by Congress under the Trade and Development Act of 2000. CBTPA extended duty-free and quota-free treatment to some apparel imported from Guatemala and other regional countries that had been excluded under previous Caribbean Basin Initiative (CBI) agreements. To qualify, the apparel had to be assembled from material made and cut in the United States or fabric made in the United States from American-made yarn.[12] Current bilateral negotiations between the United States and Central American countries, including Guatemala, to form a free trade zone referred to as the Central American Free Trade Agreement (CAFTA) will most probably expand incentives to *maquilas* to encourage companies to establish shops in the region.

Another reason for the *maquila* explosion of the mid-1980s was that USAID adopted the then small Guatemalan private trade association that promoted investment in nontraditional export production. As of 1985, the association, the Gremial de Exportadores de Productos No Tradicionales, began receiving most of its funding and technical assistance from USAID.[13] Edgar Sperisen, former GEXPRONT president, told Kurt Petersen in 1991, "We would not be anywhere close to where we are today without the support of AID. From the beginning they gave us vital and essential assistance. Indeed, the growth of nontraditional exports would be at least four times less without AID fund and supervision."[14] Although USAID today is most interested in using GEXPRONT to promote nontraditional agrarian production in preparation for CAFTA, GEXPRONT continues to coordinate and fund lobbying and technical support for the *maquila* industry.[15]

The Cerezo Arévalo government supported the U.S. trajectory of expanding nontraditional exports. Soon after taking power in 1986, President Cerezo Arévalo announced the state's National Social and Economic Reordering Plan (Programa de Reordenamiento Económico y Social; PRES), which outlined the government's support for neoliberal development. PRES sought to encourage private investment (foreign and national) by freeing up foreign exchange controls; devaluing the national currency, the quetzal(Q); and securing foreign aid to modernize both state and economic sectors. The government formed the National Export Promotion Council, composed of representatives from both the private and public sectors, to help "promote and diversify export."[16] Congress also modified the 1984 *maquila* law (Decree 24–84) to further advance *maquila* investment. Decree 24–84 had contained most of the ingredients of similar *maquila* support laws around the world—a ten-year tax holiday, suspension of export and import tariffs, and profit repatriation—but it forbade subcontracting and selling any portion of the assembled products in the domestic market.[17] The 1989 revisions in the form of the Drawback Industries Law (Decree 29–89) and Free Trade Zones Law (Decree 65–89) permitted both the private and public sectors to establish free trade zones anywhere in the country, allowing a single business to stand alone as a free trade zone. The modifications also opened the industry to unrestricted subcontracting.[18]

Keeping in mind the deep interest and support of the U.S. government in the early years of *maquila* growth, it is an interesting anomaly that the *maquila* sector in Guatemala is dominated not by U.S. manufacturers but by ones from South Korea. As of 2003, of the 217 apparel *maquilas* listed by VESTEX, 154 were owned by South Koreans; 52 by Guatemalans; 3 by Americans; and 8 by investors of other nationalities.[19] Kurt Petersen partially explains the South Korean domination by the presence of Key-Sung Cho, South Korean ambassador to Guatemala from April 1988 until July 1990. At the time of the passage of CBERA, Cho had been the director of South Korea's American Bureau, and he became convinced that CBERA was a way for Korean manufacturers to get around growing U.S. restrictions against Korean apparel imports.[20] After becoming ambassador to Guatemala, Cho lobbied Korean manufacturers about the trade and production benefits of relocating. He was aided by simultaneous rising tensions within Korean society that were fanning political and economic instability there. He successfully convinced a good number of firms to establish factories in Guatemala. The Korean Embassy in Guatemala, opened at the height of the Guatemalan military government's repression in 1977, became an active support base for Korean manufacturers when they did relocate. One former U.S. Embassy trade attaché contended that the Korean Embassy was in fact the "self-proclaimed headquarters for all Korean investors," negotiating labor settlements, contracts with subcontractors, and helping manufacturers maneuver through the Guatemalan bureaucracy.[21]

The absence of U.S. direct investment in the *maquila* industry in Guatemala, however, does not negate the prominent role that U.S. apparel companies do play in the industry. Most *maquilas* depend on contracts or subcontracts from U.S. apparel labels and produce almost exclusively for the American market. *Maquilas* located in Guatemala, for example, have produced clothing at various times for labels that include Liz Claiborne, Pierre Cardin, GAP/Old Navy, Ralph Lauren, GEAR for Sports, Jones

Apparel, J.C. Penney, Hanes, Target, and Tracy Evans, Ltd.[22] By contracting or subcontracting production, U.S.-based companies have tried to distance themselves from the everyday operations of the plant and the corresponding labor tensions. They also maintain a more flexible position in the market: shopping for the cheapest supplier, easily reducing their production when markets slow without having to pay worker compensation, and relocating production to other plants within or outside Guatemala if production conditions deteriorate.

Thus, by 2001, Central America held 11.87 percent of the market share of U.S. apparel and textile imports.[23] Though Guatemala only had 2.84 percent of the market share—behind those of Honduras and El Salvador—it had increased its production and exportation of apparel and textiles significantly in less than twenty years. The importance of this growth should be of interest not only to government planners and manufacturers but also to students of gender. As mentioned earlier, the majority of workers in the new industry were women. Certainly, the economic crisis of the late 1990s brought more men into the *maquila* factories, but women continue to dominate most areas of production. Their presence on the factory floor is not only essential to *maquila* operations but also has reverberations throughout Guatemalan society.

BIRDS FLOCK TOGETHER: GUATEMALTECAS
IN THE WORKFORCE

By the time of the *maquila* explosion in Guatemala, Guatemaltecas were already present in the workforce, not only in domestic and informal employment but also in factories. They worked in factories like ACRICASA, a Japanese-owned thread factory in Guatemala, and a few became key labor activists. But these women were still a minority before the mid-1980s.[24] Men dominated the factory floor and unions throughout the 1950s–1970s. Not only did men have the legal right to refuse to allow their wives and daughters to work outside the home, the majority of men—at least discursively—supported traditional gender constructions that highlighted the man as the breadwinner and the woman as the person in charge of domestic and childcare duties. As Don Felipe informed Santiago Bastos in the 1990s, "I prefer to work two times. Once in the morning and another in the afternoon, so that she [his wife] can dedicate herself to the family."[25]

In reality, however, as Deborah Levenson-Estrada acknowledges, gender roles were not so sharply defined: "Working-class people have lived in a gray area of gender 'imperfection.' " This means that while they never dismantled the feminine ideal, neither did they "strictly adhere to" it.[26] Rather, women's outside employment is explained away as temporary, part-time, merely help to the husband, an extension of her household chores, a means for a woman to earn a bit of spending money to buy luxury items, a way to fill her extra time, or because she is not a good student. One husband, for example, explained to Santiago Bastos:

> She was working, but with the small children, she had to quit, but sometimes she helps me from there [the house], washing and ironing [for others], or at times if someone wants to eat something, well she prepares it for them. In order to go on helping a little the situation, because it is hard . . .[27]

By not defining working women as workers, by belittling their contribution to family subsistence, by refusing to let female family members work outside the home, and by supporting the myth of the gendered public/private divide, Guatemalan men support the conditions of exploitation of female labor. Women are defined by their capacity to reproduce, not by their productive powers.

Even so, there are ample cases in which Guatemaltecas have subverted normative gender roles, taking on identities as workers, breadwinners, heads of household, and union activists, as well as mothers, daughters, and wives. Individual women have always subverted the ideal gender constructs, and indigenous families as a sector have more generally defined gender roles somewhat differently than the dominant ideal. Still, the economic crisis of the last few decades and the growth of formal-sector employment for women are leading to more radical changes in gender configurations.

In the 1970s, Guatemalan women worked, but rarely did they (or their families) identify themselves as workers. Most women and men continued to define workers as male, despite the presence of women in the factories. Women who did adjust their self-definitions to incorporate both *woman* and *worker,* and possibly even *unionist,* often did so in rather specific situations. The absence of men in the home due to political repression, economic predicaments, or choice sometimes allowed women the freedom and need to rethink their gender roles. For instance, Sonia Oliva, a union leader at ACRICASA during the 1970s, told Levenson-Estrada:

> But you know the reason I told you this tale [of how she came to live alone with a girlfriend] is to explain *how* I could get involved in the

union. There was no one at home to stop me, a woman . . . no husband, mother, father, mother-in-law, father-in-law. I was alone.[28]

Male workers and unionists had their own problems with women entering the factories. In accepting women into the factory and unions, male factory workers sometimes either placed themselves in protector or possessor roles[29] or masculinized the female activists. One man at the Ray-O-Vac battery factory, for instance, contended that

> there were many abuses, but especially against women, because in exchange for having a job they had to sleep with the managers, and they used to sit and cry and tell us about it. A committee formed to protest this, and with this the whole procedure of getting a union started.[30]

In protecting their abused co-workers, the men defended their masculinity; they replicated a component of the ideal gender construction on the factory floor (male protector, dependent weak female) and put some gender order into a nonideal situation. Thus patriarchal norms served as critical tools to help organize the male working class.

As Levenson-Estrada points out, however, once women were union members, male leaders tried to keep them in subordinate positions.

> They often did not inform women of important meetings, decisions, problems, or gossip. They asked women in unions to do "women's work," such as cooking, cleaning up, and taking notes . . . when women were notably militant or capable as trade unionists, men masculinized them.[31]

Female leaders were said to have "more pants than most men."[32] To become accepted unionists, they had to be placed within the ideal gender construction as more male than men. They were no longer ideal *women* but ideal *men*. Still, male unionists also viewed these women activists as their class comrades, fighting with them against an abusive capitalist system. Thus, male unionists maneuvered gender discourses and norms to benefit class needs while simultaneously trying to uphold patriarchal privilege.

Female activists did not always concur with all these (re)configurations of their sex. They considered themselves female workers trying to make a difference economically to their families; struggling for class needs (wages and working conditions); and trying to secure their safety, comfort, and security as women in the factory. So they fought for wage increases, better transportation to and from the factories, day cares, the right for all mothers (married and not) to celebrate Mother's Day as a paid holiday,[33] overtime pay, and other improvements. Once again, Levenson-Estrada astutely notes, "There is no 'more important' or 'prior' issue—class or gender . . . women and men do not act only out of gender. Activism stems from the multiplicity of their being, of which gender is a part."[34]

The explosion of *maquilas* in Guatemala after 1986 provided a new source of income for Guatemalan families, primarily through the employment of women. Relying on stereotypic assumptions of women, managers actively sought to employ women. Women were said to have a natural aptitude and dexterity for the intricate work of the apparel assembly plant; the smaller size of their hands was more appropriate for the sewing machines, they were more patient, and sewing was, after all, women's work. As one manager stated, "We only hire men to pack and ship. They don't have the patience or the skill to operate a machine."[35] In addition, many managers considered women to be easier to control than men, due both to cultural norms and to their inexperience in the workforce. One employer told Kurt Petersen in 1991, "Men are more likely to form unions. Women do not have this mentality. They are more prone to do what you tell them without questioning. That they are better sewers is a bonus."[36]

Managers did not consider all women ideal employees. Age, marital status, number of children, and even weight were important variables to managers. Millie Woc, a personnel manager at Este Oeste S.A., candidly explained:

> Eighteen to twenty-four is the ideal age. They should not be married because when they are married they tend to have added responsibilities. Before you know it they start to have children, which is a problem. We do not hire a woman if she has small children because it is likely they will become sick, and she will often need to go to the doctor. If a woman is large, she will likely get sick often and have to go to the doctor as well. My ideal worker is young, unmarried, healthy, thin and delicate, single, lives close, and does not have previous experience.[37]

A 1997 study by the Central American Network of Women in Solidarity with *Maquila* Workers, found that 37 percent of the *maquila* operators were women under the age of twenty-four, 12 percent of whom were under sixteen years of age.[38] This is despite the fact that the labor law (Decree 1441) sets the minimum age for children to work at fourteen years old.[39]

Thus, from the beginning, the *maquila* shop floor has been dominated by female employees but also segregated according to sex. Most women are hired as machine operators or finishers (cutting the loose threads after the cloth has been sewn), while men are placed in ironing, packing, and shipping.[40] In recent years, more men have been hired in the factories, but the majority of operators are still women.[41] While some women have been promoted to supervisor positions, most administrative and management jobs are reserved for either nationals of the country of the person/company that owns the factory or male Guatemalans. Even when they are promoted to line supervisors, the women are not always sure that the promotion is worth their while, for it requires longer hours, expects the harassment of the primarily female operators to get them to produce more and faster, and rarely brings a significant wage increase.[42]

Working conditions and wages differ greatly from one factory to another. Some are modern, clean facilities, with ample ventilation and lighting.[43] Others are located in old warehouses that have little or no ventilation and extremely poor lighting.[44] Some factories provide employees with a lunchroom and clean bathrooms and the time to use both. Other factories have a limited number of bathrooms, which are poorly maintained and to which employees have only restricted access. In addition, many factories do not have the legally required lunchroom, which means that workers are forced into the streets or onto the medians of highways to eat their quick meals. Some factories facilitate the workers' access to health care by either maintaining a physician on the premises or giving employees the time to go to the hospitals and clinics run by the state Instituto Guatemalteco Seguridad Social (Guatemalan Institute for Social Security; IGSS).[45] Other managers, however, ignore the law that requires them to sign up employees for IGSS services, or if they do register their workers, they often refuse to give the women permission to visit IGSS facilities. Some factories pay the minimum wage—in 2003 set at Q420 (approximately $78) a month—but many do not.[46] Few pay overtime even though they require workers to work much longer than the legal six-day, seven-hours-a-day workweek.[47] Some grant paid vacations and holidays and severance pay, also dictated by the Labor Code,[48] but many do so only if pressured by employees and their advocates. In general, women report working under worse conditions than men, and indigenous women say that they receive harsher treatment than mestiza women.[49]

Both men and women face poor working conditions within the *maquila* industry, but Guatemalan women are also discriminated against because of their reproductive status. Again, the discrimination they face is similar to that of female *maquila* workers throughout the South. As elsewhere, the persistence of some of these practices in Guatemala highlights not only global industrial but also local patriarchal norms. Several organizations have documented the ways in which *maquilas* discriminate against women based on their reproductive status. Women are often grilled before hiring about their sex lives, how many children they have, if they are pregnant, and about their family responsibilities. It is also quite common to require that they obtain a negative pregnancy test before being hired. The pregnancy test is sometimes conducted by an in-house medical practitioner, and at other times, the prospective employee is required to pay a private facility to have the test performed. Both testing formats violate the woman's right to privacy. A twenty-three-year-old factory worker, for example, told researchers in 1999 that when she applied for her job, she was told to return when she had proof that she was not pregnant. "She went to a laboratory and paid Q20 [$2.60] for the test. When she returned two days later, she was hired."[50] Sandra Chicop was only fourteen years old when she applied for a job in a *maquila*.

> In the interview for the job, they asked her age, how many siblings she had, how many children she had, whether she had to support anyone on her salary, and if she was pregnant. "They sent me first to a room, there's a lady doctor, and she touched my stomach. She said, you're expecting, she insisted that I had been with a man, and I told her no. And then she examined me again, and said no. And I was an adolescent, I didn't know anything about any of that."[51]

International rights organizations have campaigned against these discriminatory actions. While some factory administrators admit to the illegality of the testing procedures, others are adept at ignoring criticisms. When questioned by Human Rights Watch, for instance, one factory manager explained that pregnancy status is determined "in order to take into consideration the woman with respect to licenses [to leave work], or any other need she may have. The question is not for hiring directly, but rather in consideration of the person."[52]

If a woman becomes pregnant while working in a *maquila* in Guatemala, she may find herself without a job, although recent research shows that "direct dismissal of pregnant workers is less common now than it was in the past."[53] The Labor Code contends that if a woman informs her employer of her pregnancy and provides a doctor's note within two months confirming her situation, she cannot be fired unless her dismissal is first approved by a judge.[54] The law is not strictly administered, however, and pregnant *maquila* workers still face illegal dismissals. On the other hand, if a pregnant worker is not dismissed, she often faces other illegal sanctions, since factory owners rarely grant all of the maternity and postnatal benefits guaranteed by the law. The Labor Code ensures access to health care for all employees,[55] grants pregnant workers eighty-four days of paid maternity leave, and secures them ten months of breast-feeding rights (remunerated time away from their jobs to breast-feed their infants). Employers have been known to deny pregnant women and postnatal mothers access to health care—even though they deduct the employee contribution from each paycheck—refuse to allow them time to breast-feed their children, or rebuff requests for on-site day-care facilities, required by law of any factory with thirty or more female employees.[56]

Women working in the *maquilas* in Guatemala have also reported sexual harassment, being forced to have sexual relations with supervisors in order to get or keep jobs, being humiliated or intimidated by male administrators and workers, and being hit and beaten by supervisors for perceived misbehavior. Another inequality within the factories, less spoken about and documented but still relevant, is the inequity of wages based on sex. Women are hired for the lowest-paying jobs in the factory. In addition, when performing similar jobs, women are usually paid less. Government agencies are only now starting the process of adding sex as a criterion when collecting statistical data, so statistical information on wages tabulated by gender is still largely unavailable.[57] Still, survey data points to significant wage discrepancies between sexes. In 1992 interviews with forty-five female and male *maquila* workers conducted by AVANCSO, the women, as a group, were the poorest paid. Of the thirty-seven women interviewed, twenty-six were employed as machine operators being paid between Q101 and Q550 a month. The only male operator received between Q701 and Q705 a month. Of the eight male workers interviewed, all received wages between Q251 and Q750, with three of these earning more than any women queried, between Q601 and Q750.[58] In addition, the *aguinaldo* (Christmas bonus) and *bono 14* (annual bonus) are based on monthly salary earnings, so women usually take home smaller bonuses.

Maquila owners hire women precisely because they can be paid less than men, and women can be paid less because of the inequity of gender norms. The maintenance of these social norms thus becomes critical to *maquila* employers to maintain the cheap labor force that secures them their profits. Employers thus resort to numerous tactics to replicate the society's methods of controlling women's behavior. Studies throughout the South have adroitly shown how patriarchal structures have been nourished by *maquila* owners: women are encouraged to compete for the manager's attention by dressing in certain ways, and bathing suit contests are held at company picnics. Female workers are also treated like school-aged children while on the job: they are not allowed to get out of their seats or go to the bathroom without permission; they cannot talk with one another, are not allowed to eat or drink at their desks, and are locked out of the factory (and docked a day's wage) if they arrive a few minutes late in the morning. Like some men at home, the male managers and supervisors use intimidation, responsibility, and paternalist support to control the bodies (and work) of women.

In Guatemala, the managers of Korean establishments have been most ridiculed locally for using language differences,[59] feigning ignorance of Guatemalan laws, claiming the superiority of Korean workers,[60] and taking advantage of cultural variations to exploit Guatemalteca labor in the *maquila*. In reality, however, *maquila* employers, whatever their nationality, use comparable tactics: applying divide-and-conquer strategies that ridicule indigenous women and grant special favors to the "prettiest" workers, ignoring rulings by the labor courts that favor workers, and demanding unquestioning adherence to the demands of factory supervisors. If individual workers "misbehave," they are dismissed.

In addition, employers have been loath to tolerate unions. As Carlos Arias of Cádiz S.S. explained to Kurt Petersen in the early 1990s, "This industry is very delicate and intolerant of disruptions. . . . Unions by nature disrupt and, hence, must be avoided."[61] If a union has tried to form, employers have used a combination of bribery, co-optation, and repression to discourage workers from joining. One manager purportedly put up a picture on a factory bulletin board of tortured corpses with the caption "Look what happens to unionists."[62] At times factory owners will offer bonuses to those who reject attempts to organize unions or fund the formation of worker-employer Solidarismo investment associations that tout a nonpolitical solution to workers' problems.[63] If none of these tactics, or a combination thereof, works to the satisfaction of the employer, the factory is closed and reopened in a new location.

In addition to employer tactics, the reactive rather than pro-active policies of the Guatemalan government against exploitative policies in the factories have made it difficult for workers to organize. In the early 1990s, a factory owner described the Ministry of Labor as a "little mosquito . . . Sometimes a pest but easy to swat away."[64] Although post–peace accords legislative reforms have bolstered their legal powers, Ministry of Labor officials are still viewed by factory owners more as pesky gnats than enforcers with teeth. And despite the requirements of the Labor Code that it actively protect the rights of laborers, the Ministry rarely initiates an independent investigation of possible industry abuses.[65] Instead, individual workers who feel that they have been mistreated or discriminated against can make complaints to one of three Ministry divisions: visitations (complaints about current employers), conciliation (postemployment complaints), and mediation (public employees and the most "difficult" cases).[66] If enough evidence is presented, a labor investigator arranges to speak to the factory manager. Sometimes this meeting takes place in the presence of the worker, a most intimidating situation for any woman who is still employed by the company in question. Sanctions, if issued—which they rarely are—tend to be light. For instance, when two *maquila* supervisors were sentenced to thirty days in jail for physically abusing workers, their sentences were reduced to Q5 (83¢) a day, plus civil penalties of Q75 ($12.50).[67] Even if Ministry employees had the political will to uphold the law, the lack of available training and funding constrains them. In 1994, the Sección de Promoción y Capacitación de la Mujer Trabajadora (Section for the Promotion and Training of the Woman Worker) was created under the Ministry to help train agency employees about gender issues and to advise women workers of their rights. Lacking the funding and support, however, the office has done little of either since being formed.[68] In 2003, the Ministry of Labor was budgeted some Q58,347,599, one of the lowest-funded ministries.[69] The inadequate funding ensures that the Ministry will continue, at least for the time being, to be ill staffed and to lack the necessary provisions for the operation of an efficient office. For example, in 2001, there were only two agency lawyers to help complainants make their cases through the courts, and investigators had only three cars to use for official business.[70]

Despite discouragement from employers and government officials, *maquila* workers have mobilized and organized to fight for their rights as workers and working women since 1986. Similar to those female factory workers in the 1970s, women in this second phase of unionization are mobilizing around a popular feminist ideology, which refuses to separate or prioritize gender and class. Still, the second phase of unionization is taking place under very different conditions than the first, and they are affecting its form and context. Repression remains a fact of life in Guatemala, but the levels and the depth of the violence are not what they were in the 1970s. A body of law, both international and domestic, provides a basis for defining the rights of workers and women. While this legislation is not always upheld by state sectors in Guatemala, it provides a critical moral and tactical foundation for unionists. In addition, the sheer numbers and importance of women in the factories today have forced the male-dominated unions of the 1970s to retool themselves with regard to gender politics.[71] The growth of a feminist movement in Guatemala has also lent support to female workers in the *maquila*. Three organizations, specifically, the Asociación de Mujeres en Solidaridad (Association of Women in Solidarity; AMES), the Grupo Femenino Pro-Mejoramiento de la Familia (GRUFEPROMEFAM), and the Centro para Acción Legal en Derechos Humanos (CALDH), all have programs to educate and assist *maquila* women in obtaining their rights.[72] Finally, since the mid-1980s, women have taken on a new and decisive role in the formal economy. Though women have always been important in the nation's economic development, the current stage of female proletarianization is essential for economic restructuring.

This said, however, unionization drives in the *maquilas* since 1986 have still been difficult, brutally repressed, and often unsuccessful in achieving their modest goals. In 2003, there were only two unions operating in the *maquila* industry. Despite the fact that the Guatemalan Constitution and the Labor Code ensure workers the freedom to organize, the laws have remained woefully unenforced except in a few rare cases when heavy international pressure has been applied on both the Guatemalan government and transnational producers.

One of the most well-known unionization cases in Guatemala was that of the workers at the Phillips-Van Heusen (PVH) apparel-for-export plant, Camisas Modernas. Workers struggled for six years in the 1990s to obtain legal recognition of their union and then to force PVH to negotiate a collective bargaining contract. In seeking to unionize, workers denounced widespread violations, including illegal employment of minors, failure to pay the legal minimum wage, refusal to enroll workers in the national health program as required by law, forced overtime, failure to provide legally required vacation pay and annual bonuses, abuse by supervisors, and extensive homework. They also complained that pro-union workers were being illegally fired, harassed, and intimidated.

In 1991, PVH workers obtained the support of labor and grassroots organizations in the United States, increasingly concerned with the movement of jobs to countries like Guatemala with weak records of protecting the rights of workers. In 1992, the union STECAMOSA (Sindicato de Trabajadores de la Empresa CAMOSA; Union of Workers at the CAMOSA Company) became the first union in the Guatemalan *maquila* industry to receive legal recognition. It was no coincidence that the recognition came only days before the Guatemalan government was to testify before the U.S. Trade Representative in response to petitions from support groups in the United States that charged Guatemala with the failure to advance worker rights.

Despite STECAMOSA's legal status, PVH refused to negotiate a contract with the union. After several years of increasingly deteriorating working conditions, the union initiated a new campaign in 1996 with an enlarged international support base led by the International Textile, Garment, and Leather Workers Federation (ITGLWF) and its North American affiliate, the Union of Needle Trades, Industrial, and Textile Employees (UNITE!). PVH management continued to resist but finally agreed—under pressure from U.S. rights organizations—to negotiate, and a contract was signed in August 1997.[73] The contract secured the adherence of the company to requirements regarding the minimum wage, forty-four-hour workweek, overtime pay, and health-care availability. Less than seventeen months after signing the collective bargaining contract with STECAMOSA, PVH shut the factory, claiming the loss of a major client. Critics of the corporation have countered that the closure had nothing to do with the financial stability of the company but was engineered to break the union. Data seems to support their contention: PVH did not reduce its production in Guatemala after closing the plant but merely dispersed its contracts to independently owned *maquilas*. PVH shipments from its contractors in Guatemala and Central America in fact increased immediately after the closing of the Camisas Modernas plant.[74] The PVH factory was the last U.S. apparel company to directly manage a factory in Guatemala. Since its closure, American apparel labels have instead come to depend wholly on contracting and subcontracting agreements with independently owned factories.

The PVH case points to an implicit agreement between various international and domestic sectors and the interests of transnational corporations. At the same time that the PVH was violating the rights of Camisas Modernas workers—acts at least passively supported by the Guatemalan government—PVH corporate leaders were helping to set U.S. and industry policies toward *maquilas*. PVH participated on the White House's Apparel Industry Partnership, a task force formed by the Clinton administration in 1996 to examine sweatshop abuses; assisted in the writing of a code of conduct for the industry; and helped to form the Fair Labor Association (FLA) in 1998 to monitor the conduct of sweatshops contracted or subcontracted by American labels to produce clothing for the U.S. market. In addition, Bruce Klatsky, PVH's Chief Executive Officer since 1994, has been a member of the board of directors of Human Rights Watch, an internationally established human rights organization, since 1996. Although Human Rights Watch played a critical role in getting Klatsky and the PVH to the bargaining table in 1997, the organization was more or less silent after the closing of the factory in 1998. In fact, a 2003 study of sex discrimination in the Guatemalan labor force by Human Rights Watch barely mentions the PVH case and only does so in benign ways.[75]

Neither Klatsky's work with Human Rights Watch nor PVH's participation on the White House task force or its support of FLA and the code of conduct ensured Guatemalan workers that PVH would uphold Guatemalan labor laws. While international pressure clearly helped STECA-MOSA obtain legal status and pushed PVH to enter into collective bargaining negotiations, it did not secure the long-term health and longevity of the union or labor reforms in Guatemala. This is not to criticize the international solidarity movement but to indicate a possible flaw in a strategy that depends too heavily on antiglobalization appeals (or Mohanty's strategic international feminism) to reform the *maquila* industry. Without the support of the Guatemalan state for reforms, it is difficult for labor to sustain victories. One might therefore rationally conclude that a strong and motivated state is necessary, possibly in conjunction with international pressure, to protect domestic labor rights against international capitalistic interests.[76]

This said, the politics of CAFTA has further encouraged the link between Guatemalan unionists and the international solidarity movement. For example, in the early twenty-first century, antiglobalization sectors in the United States united with workers at the Choi Shin and Cimatextiles apparel-for-export plants, twin factories in Villa Nueva, Guatemala, to help them obtain a collective bargaining contract from their Korean owners, Choi and Shin, in July 2003. There are many similarities between the PVH and Choi Shin cases but also one critical difference: the role played by the Guatemalan government in the latter case. After the unions Sindicato de Trabajadores de Choi Shin (Choi Shin Workers Union; SITRACHOI) and Sindicato de Trabajadores de Cimatextiles (Cimatextiles Workers Union, SITRACIMA) gained legal status in July 2001 and set their goal on a collective bargaining agreement, union activists faced death threats, illegal dismissals, rape, mob violence, and other forms of intimidation. They sought and secured the intervention of the ITGLWF, the Guatemalan union federation FESTRAS (Federación Sindical de Trabajadores de la Alimentación, Agro-Industrias y Similares; Federation of Food and Allied Workers Union), Guatemalan women's and rights organizations, the American-based advocacy group US/Labor Education in the Americas Project, and the Fair Labor Asso-

ciation. All of these entities lent technical and legal help, capacity training, moral support, and/or lobbying assistance to the union. The *maquila*
owners, however, steadfastly refused to negotiate with union leaders until
the Guatemalan government threatened to withdraw the company's export license if it did not negotiate contracts with the union, reinstate illegally fired union members, and work with the union to resolve problems
in the factories.

Since the government had generally failed in the past to side with unionists in their disputes with factory owners, the actions of the Guatemalan
government in the Choi Shin case are only explicable within the context of
the free trade negotiations occurring at the time. In the midst of CAFTA
negotiations, the AFL-CIO and International Labor Rights Fund filed a
petition with the U.S. Trade Representative in December 2002 requesting
that Guatemala be excluded from the U.S. Generalized System of Preferences for continuing "to systematically violate workers' rights to freedom
of association and collective bargaining." The timing of the petition put
pressure on both the U.S. and Guatemalan governments to "throw a bone
to labor."[77] Gloria Cordova, the General Secretary of SITRACIMA, the
Cimatextiles factory union, concurred:

> We know that if the free trade agreement didn't exist, this [the success-
> ful negotiation of a collective bargaining contract] would never have
> happened. We know that this action is the result of the complaints that
> we made on a national and international level. Guatemala has to protect
> its image that it defends labor rights. It seems that the free trade nego-
> tiations are stalling over the poor reputation Guatemala has received at
> the international level over the case of Choi Shin. So that is what moti-
> vated the proposal to sanction the companies and oblige the collective
> bargaining agreement.[78]

While CAFTA negotiations and the threat of excluding the country from
free trade benefits may have prodded a positive response from the Guatemala government in the Choi Shin case, activists are unsure whether state
support will be withdrawn once CAFTA is in place.[79]

CONCLUSIONS

Although there were many more Guatemalan women working in factories
in 2003 than there were in 1977, they still faced some of the same restrictions in their private and public lives. The feminine ideal—women caring
for the home and family—remained firmly entrenched, though not strictly

adhered to. Female *maquila* workers thus continued to work double and triple shifts in the factory and at home; *maquila* management employed gendered tactics to control the behavior of employees on the job; and husbands and fathers, while no longer legally able to restrain a wife or daughter from working, still wielded the power over the movements of family women. Organizers and researchers wanting to talk with female *maquila* workers in their homes, for example, in most cases still had to get the permission of husbands and fathers to talk with the women.[80] Women who joined unions without the permission of their families continued to face an uphill battle at home and in the factory. While union federations, still dominated by men, had begun to see the practicality of organizing the new female proletarian base, female workers and activists persistently encountered the gender double standard in framing and implementing union demands.[81]

In 2004, conditions are improving for women working in factories, but many still need to be changed. Some of the most restrictive laws against working women have been repealed: they now do not have to get the permission of fathers and husbands to work outside the home, maternity and postnatal benefits are legally ensconced, and employers cannot legally discriminate against women in the hiring process. But though these legislative reforms exist on paper, as we have seen, they are by no means effectively enforced. One can rationalize this lack of enforcement as a sign of weak governance, corrupt bureaucracy, and/or a financially strapped state—all of which are no doubt true—yet the dilemma of global capital needing to reconfigure gender roles while relying on patriarchal norms to control cheap female labor also plays a part in producing this rather volatile situation. The *maquila* industry needs women to be freed somewhat from family and societal patriarchal norms to work long hours in the factories, but it continues to depend on some of those same norms to maintain a cheap and malleable labor force.

In addition to changes in workforce composition and labor legislation, another major change has been the mobilization of an international solidarity movement linked not only by political ideals like those of the support movements of earlier times, but by united economic goals as well. The working conditions in Guatemalan *maquilas* producing for the U.S. market have direct effects (both negative and positive) on the lives of U.S. workers and consumers. The move by the U.S. and Central American governments to sign the Central American Free Trade Agreement has brought these shared interests to the forefront for workers in both regions. The partnership between the two groups of workers has already reaped some benefits for Guatemalan workers, but without the backing of a strong Guatemalan state, benefits may be short lived.

It is impossible for workers or employers of *maquilas* in Guatemala to fully separate gender from their economic activities. In different ways and to various extents, both groups utilize, abuse, and struggle against gender norms in the workplace to build or control working communities, to organize or destroy unions, and to regulate production. The multiple and contradictory uses of gender by various participants in *maquila* manufacturing is opening up the topic for discussion by working women in Guatemala. Working families in Guatemala have long been able to simultaneously confirm yet not completely adhere to ideal gender norms, but as women choose or are forced by economic conditions to "take themselves seriously as workers," they will begin to reexamine and reshape "the roles into which they are cast at home and in society, where they are not considered real workers."[82] The importance of their role in the current economic restructuring in Guatemala and their integration into the formal economy may lead to just such rethinking.

Mujeres organizadas y a título individual marcharon el pasado
29 de junio (2004) en la ciudad capital para repudiar, una vez
más, la creciente ola de asesinatos de guatemaltecas.[1]

— LAURA E. ASTURIAS

As the previous chapters have illustrated, the relationship between globalization and the women's movement in Guatemala is explicable only as
a complicated dialectical trajectory. Globalization is leading Guatemaltecas to renegotiate their positions and relations within both their private and public lives. It is also encouraging changes—NGOization, institutionalization, clientelism—in the women's movement as the movement
adjusts to neoliberal economic and political reforms. While international
discourses are influencing the shapes of new gender constructs in Guatemala, they are not doing so without the consultation of, and at times
the rejection by, local constructs. In fact, Guatemalteca organizations are
helping to localize global constructions of gender identity. As we have
seen, Guatemaltecas—political activists, femocrats, workers, and lesbians—are developing counterdiscourses in resistance to both traditional
patriarchal structures and various alternative global constructions of gender. In the process, they are forcing a rethinking of women's roles in the
national body politic. Still, this study also illustrates the mixed consequences of resistance and the resiliency of the patriarchy. The story about
gender in Guatemala is not—nor will it ever be—over. A discussion of the
dialectics of gendered violence in 2003 demonstrates this unfinished trajectory, the malleability of the patriarchy, and the strength of resistance
discourses.

REASSESSING VIOLENCE AND RESISTANCE

As Guatemalans prepared to go to the polls in November 2003 to elect
a new president, a vice president, 158 congressional representatives, 20

representatives to the Central American Parliament, and 331 mayors, violence escalated. In the six months preceding the elections, twenty political leaders and activists were murdered, thirteen received death threats, another thirteen survived gunshot wounds, eleven were victims of physical and psychological intimidation, nine had their homes or vehicles fired upon, and three had their homes broken into.[2] In addition, at least sixteen journalists were targets of threats and intimidation. But violence against political activists was not the only type of violence to increase; violence against women also swelled. Between March 2003 and October 2003, 291 women were assassinated, 78 kidnapped, 20 raped, and 11 tortured.[3] Many of the bodies of those killed showed signs of sexual abuse and torture. Although the majority of these cases were not identified as politically motivated, knowing what we do about the strategic manipulation of gender for political purposes, we need to rethink the preelectoral violence through a gendered lens. Such an analysis not only shows a decided link between the two kinds of violence but demonstrates ways in which the patriarchy is both being threatened by resistance discourses and remaking itself within the new global era.

Feminists have long noted the relationship of the state to patriarchal power and gendered violence. Susan Rae Peterson likened the state to a protection racket that promises to protect the "good woman" but punish the "bad ones" who question masculinist constructions of gender.[4] Building on this protectionist racket analogy, Iris Marion Young associates the "particular logic of masculism" with "the position of male head of household as a protector of the family, and, by extension, with masculine leaders and risk takers as protectors of a population."[5] In Hobbesian tradition, she says, the logic of masculinist protection maintains that in the uncertainty of the state of nature, "good" men/leaders will protect their women and children/citizens, while "bad" men/leaders are liable to attack/abuse. According to this logic, "virtuous masculinity depends on its constitutive relation to the presumption of evil others."[6] A bargain is implicit in the masculinist protector role: either submit to my governance or all the bad men out there may get you.

Although Young's focus is the rise of the security state in the post-9/11 United States,[7] much of her analysis is applicable to understanding recent gendered electoral violence in Guatemala. In the 2003 elections, male candidates strategically used violence—either by encouraging it or rhetorically exploiting it—to establish themselves in protector roles; they were "good" men who would protect female citizens against the evil ones who wanted to attack them.[8] It was sometimes difficult, however, for an outsider to differentiate the defender from the assailant.

The violence of the 2003 campaign is usually divided into two unrelated parts: political and nonpolitical violence. Violence against party activists is placed in the first category and that against women into the second. The Guatemalan Republican Front (Frente Republicano Guatemalteco; FRG), the party of then President Alfonso Portillo and presidential candidate Efraín Ríos Montt, is most often blamed for the rise in political violence, whereas illegal elements—youth gangs, drug dealers, petty criminals—are held responsible for violence against women and other individuals in society. But in reality, the two kinds of violence are largely inseparable; in most cases, both are gendered and politically motivated. The FRG sought to create a situation of insecurity prior to the elections to stop the political opposition from trying to keep Ríos Montt off the ballot[9] and to convince the urban and rural masses of the need for a security candidate such as Ríos Montt to restore postelectoral stability. To accomplish these goals, the party relied on clientelist politics[10] and organized crime,[11] ties to both having been forged during the country's authoritarian period.

Though recognized by many as a component of the political strategy of the Frente Republicano Guatemalteco (FRG), the political violence surrounding the electoral campaign is rarely considered for its gendered contexts. While not always obviously so, these violent incidents were nonetheless gendered in that they upheld masculinist constructs of power. In October 2003, for example, Rigoberta Menchú appeared in front of the Corte de Constitucionalidad (Court of Constitutionality; CC) to petition against allowing Ríos Montt to run for president because of violations against human rights perpetrated by his government in 1982–1983. Inside the court, Menchú was met by more than two hundred FRG "sympathizers" who pushed and jeered at her with comments such as, "Andá a vender tomates a La Terminal."[12] Though this clash was politically motivated, such FRG taunts were also racist and sexist: an indigenous woman should be selling tomatoes in the marketplace, not petitioning the courts on matters of party politics. This and other attacks on the political opposition almost always carried multiple messages tied to race, class, and gender, not just political ideology, thus appealing to the complexity of layered identity constructs in Guatemalan society.

The FRG also sought to create a situation of insecurity, or rather, one of FRG-regulated state of nature,[13] by encouraging the use of violence by gangs, ex–Civil Patrol members, militarized groups, and corrupt sectors against civil society. In doing so, the party—under the slogan "Security, Well-Being, and Justice"—relied on a logic of masculinist protection similar to that explored by Young; a situation of insecurity would necessitate the election of a "good" man to protect civil society.[14] Violence against civil society, and specifically against "vulnerable" women, fostered a sense of insecurity; after all, if women were threatened, the very foundation of the masculinist system was endangered.[15] There is no proof, and it would be extremely doubtful, that the FRG urged its supporters to directly attack women. But this is not the point. In a state of insecurity, masculinist logic dictates that "bad" men will attack "good" women, and "good" men/leaders must come forward to protect them. Creating a need for a security candidate necessitates a "vulnerable" population in a situation of insecurity. A threat to masculinist norms helped push male factory workers to organize in the 1970s, and the FRG hoped that this new threat would lead to the election of Ríos Montt in 2003.

Their hope was not realized, however, because on November 9, 2003, Guatemalans went to the polls and soundly defeated Ríos Montt. His electoral loss can be understood partly as the result of the bungling of the protectionist strategy in the hands of the FRG, but it also should be recognized as a vote by Guatemaltecas against the "particular logic of masculinism." First, the FRG failed to disassociate itself as the creator of the state of insecurity, and therefore it became difficult to portray itself as the savior from that so-called state of nature. Too many Guatemalans directly linked the rising violence with the FRG, thus the FRG became for many the "bad" men that an elected protector ("good" man) should combat. In fact, other political parties fanned the public's sense of insecurity to portray themselves as the authentic parties of security and "good men/leaders" who would combat violence against women.[16] The United States, no doubt, also influenced the electoral returns against Ríos Montt by making it well known that it did not view Ríos Montt as an appropriate partner in the future creation of the CAFTA. Perhaps the most interesting development in the 2003 elections, however, was that women and youths voted in concert against Ríos Montt.[17] It would be premature to make any lofty claims that Guatemaltecas were taking a concerted stand against the "masculinist protection racket" with their vote or that a gender electoral divide exists in Guatemalan electoral politics, but the vote may signal an initial step toward demanding an integral, rather than procedural, approach to democratization; populations not considered politically important in the past used their vote decisively to shape the future of national politics.

Guatemala, however, is a long way from constructing an integral democracy. The state thus far has failed to properly implement the peace accords and close the wounds of the civil war.[18] Only one party in the 2003 elections, the URNG, included the implementation of the peace accords in its platform; the others claimed erroneously that the peace accords hold no interest for the majority of the Guatemalan population.[19] As in other countries with similarly violent recent pasts, analysts consider societal healing to be a minimal starting point for building democracy. But the means to that healing are complex and somewhat elusive; how is national memory constructed, what is the relationship between voice and truth, how can justice be deconstructed, and who is to blame for past injustices?[20]

Academic and popular debates of national healing often extend the nation/woman analogy; the abused nation and the battered woman must both go through a therapeutic process to close their wounds and move forward. The abused nation is symbolized in the body of an abused woman. Some explanations of national and individual abuse still carry a suggestion of "blaming the victim"—maybe the rape victim should not have been jogging in the park after dark, the woman with the black eye should not have provoked her drunken husband, the indigenous community should not have supported the subversives. In general, however, there has been a significant move away from "the victim-blaming atmosphere of past decades," and instead, the individual and/or nation victim is portrayed in opposite fashion, as "pure, innocent, blameless, and free of problems (before abuse) . . . in juxtaposition with the perpetrator as evil monster."[21] Or "she" is portrayed as a "survivor," a term evoking heroic adaptation. Nevertheless, reminiscent of other labels, the victim or survivor labels consolidate all "victims/survivors" into an undifferentiated mass.[22] They are equally traumatized, treatable, and courageous, whether they are individuals or nations.

In this way, emphasis is put on the pain and suffering of victims and their heroic attempts to fight off their attackers and recover from the assaults, but a multitude of alternative realities are ignored as the victim/survivor is essentialized. To receive moral, legal, or medical assistance, victims/survivors learn that they must present themselves as convincing victims or survivors. Successful role-playing, however, can lead to revictimization, not justice. For example, psychologist Sharon Lamb tells the story of one rape victim in the United States who, faced with having to go through a second trial after the first ended in a hung jury, told an interviewer, "I was just going to have to lose it . . . The jury wanted someone hysterical on the stand; they were gonna get one."[23] Lamb notes that the societal definition of the ideal victim in the United States is "polite, composed, deferential, and overcome by tears only when recalling her rape."[24] Thus in order to accomplish one justice, the "victim" felt that she had to endure another injustice.

Indigenous women face a similar victimization/survivorization conundrum in Guatemala. Essentialized, they must all be Rigoberta Menchús: articulate, political, and impassioned spokeswomen for the indigenous people in Guatemala who survived unbelievable personal hardships during the war. But can even Rigoberta Menchú live up to the ideal? The international human rights community and social movement activists in Guatemala helped to make Menchú the face of the ideal survivor/victim of repression to bring attention to the enormous injustices being perpetrated against the Guatemalan people. In support of their cause, indigenous women throughout the country were encouraged—directly or indirectly—to emulate Menchú's representation for the public. Like the rape victim described by Lamb, however, to be a "victim/survivor" worthy of "justice," Menchú (and all indigenous women) must maintain her victim's voice. Consequently, the objective of the political opposition has become to challenge and discredit Menchú as a victim/survivor, thereby weakening the validity of the demands of the entire community. Claiming that her testimonial is filled with lies and half-truths and that she was a member of a left-wing guerrilla organization, her detractors argue that she was not innocent, pure, or blameless during the war, and by association, neither were other indigenous women.[25] In many ways, Menchú and indigenous women throughout the country have become the targets of constant revictimization as detractors try to destroy their victim/survivor status—a status encouraged by the larger world community as a means of obtaining some type of moral, legal, and/or financial assistance.

The victim/survivor label has put indigenous women in a difficult bind in the postwar period. Though the labels may prove helpful in winning legal cases against the perpetrators of the violence, they may also help secure patriarchal ideologies in postwar discourses and policies. Cynthia Enloe notes that in postwar countries around the world, "Narrow, war-referenced categories into which many women are placed by journalists and decision-makers—even categories that seem to valorize some women

—can become the basis for crafting patriarchal and militarized public policies."[26] We have already seen the tendency of indigenous women and Guatemaltecas in general to be vulnerable-ized by legal reforms, unions, and electoral politics. A status of vulnerability creates the need for the male protectorate and supports the subordination of Guatemalteca demands to security issues.

While stressing the vulnerability of female victims/survivors of both domestic and state violence, postwar reforms have also promoted the depoliticization of gendered abuses. Again, Sharon Lamb's observations of domestic violence are relevant to our study of both domestic and national violence in Guatemala. Lamb maintains that by concentrating on the pathology of domestic abuse and victimhood, the field of psychology has depoliticized abuse, focusing the solution onto "individual therapy and individual redress through the law and police" rather than upon societal explanations and solutions.[27] Relief for the victim/survivor thus comes from individualized and nonpolitical sources aided by the professional abuse counselor. Extending these observations to violence at the national level, if an abusive situation is explained as the result of a psychotic, monstrous dictator, then the solution becomes not one of socioeconomic or even political reforms, but simply the removal and punishment of the psychopathic dictator. The solution is largely a procedural one focused on a trial and punishment of one individual rather than an examination of socioeconomic and political structures. Ríos Montt may soon face such a situation. Because of his electoral loss, he no longer has political immunity granted to him as a member of Congress, and some human rights groups have expressed a desire to bring him to trial for human rights violations. Certainly the trial and conviction of Ríos Montt would be a victory for victims/survivors of the civil war and civil society in general, but it could also be used to depoliticize historical memory of the war. Would a conviction of the "monster" and "pathological" former dictator help the state explain and put the war behind it, allowing it to permanently ignore the more socioeconomic and political explanations for the war outlined in the peace accords? Or would it provide a venue for victims/survivors to galvanize support for political reforms and justice?

Justice is obviously a contested analytical term, one used mercilessly by political foes of all shades. In places like Guatemala, which have experienced such intense repression in their recent pasts, justice is irrevocably linked to social memory. What do people who lived through such times remember and how do they tell their stories? The testimonial, like that of Rigoberta Menchú, has been praised by some as a way to provide a voice for the voiceless to tell their stories of oppression and violence, but it has been criticized by others as political propaganda. Elizabeth Jelin maintains that the testimonial is important because, as a process of re-membering, it helps those involved to simultaneously erase and create distances between themselves and the event and between themselves and the Other.[28] It thus provides a bridge between the "survivor" and the Other while bringing together multiple interpretations of the event through the survivor, editor, and reader. But just as we have learned that repression is often gendered, memories and the building of social memory are also gendered; different women experienced the events of war differently and remember those times through "feminine," classed, and ethnic eyes. The constructing of a national memory thus must take into account the memories/constructs of men and women from all ethnic, class, political, and geographical positions. Only from diversity can justice be defined and solutions sought.

For most feminists, accordingly, justice has an economic component. Women, they argue, receive less pay for doing the same work as men, are employed in the lowest-paying jobs, and head the majority of the poorest families. Feminist critiques of gender-blind development, along with Women in Development (WID), Women and Development (WAD), and Gender and Development (GAD) strategies,[29] succeeded in getting gender onto development agendas. Still, the mainstream development practices that evolved often did little more than "add women and stir."[30] Despite the dedication of many Guatemaltecas to the cause of economic equity, weaknesses in the conceptualization and practices of development in an era of globalization reduced the transformative impacts of their work. Boxed into development labels and set institutional spaces, Guatemaltecas became clients, femocrats, service providers, NGO organizers, and development professionals working within institutional cultures not always in accord with the objectives of the women's movement or with those of individual women. This is not to say that Guatemaltecas lacked agency or were pawns of the system. It does mean, however, that although Guatemaltecas brought their diverse perspectives, skills, and knowledge to the institutions they formed and participated in, institutional and larger systemic needs also shaped the discourses and actions of women and the women's movement. The relationships and changes that ensued were thus dialectically complex in nature.

RESISTING DOMINANT DISCOURSES

Globalization, in many ways, set the stage for rethinking state-civil societal relations in Guatemala as well as relationships between local and global communities. On the one hand, interest in modernization sent the Guatemalan state and the international community scurrying to moderate norms and constructs considered productivity limiting. In regard to women, modernization required that women go off to work, not have as many children, and provide political support for the neoliberal state. Consequently, new spaces—very limited and specific—were opened to the participation of women. Guatemaltecas have struggled to use the spaces offered by modernization to push for more transformative changes, stretching constructions of sexuality to include lesbian desires, gendering discussions of violence, and struggling for rights in the workplace. The results of these negotiations between the neoliberal state and women have been new legislation, state agencies, employment opportunities, and political powers for women. At the same time, laws, agencies, employers, and political structures have preserved the patriarchy.

The process of negotiating modernization has also radically affected the shape, form, and content of the women's movement. While the movement grew rapidly in numbers and visibility, it also moved from oppositional politics to "policy-focused activities, issue-specialization, and resource concentration among the more technically adept, transnationalized and professionalized."[31]

These developments increased tensions in the 1990s along traditional ethnic and class lines. By the turn of the twenty-first century, however, women had begun to build strategic bridges across ethnic, class, and geographical divides. Just as the bridge making of testimonials, according to Jelin, may provide some of the psychological work for both the survivor and others to reconsider state repression and each other, the bridge building across differences occurring now within the women's movement is helping women to rethink the movement, its organization, and its objectives. In the process, women are asking a series of important questions: By doing policy work, are women helping to transform societal gender constructs or assisting the state to impose its neoliberal agenda? Are institutional changes restructuring the patriarchy or merely "stripping the word 'gender' of its political and transformational significance?"[32] Do service projects address the needs and desires of the women they are meant to assist? How can women design more appropriate strategies, given shifting political and economic environments? They are debating the contours of the nation they would like to construct but also asking, "Can the master's tools dismantle the master's house?"[33]

These discussions are starting to give birth to counterdiscourses, which can be means to resist power, according to some theorists and activists. Challenging some of the tenants of globalization, Guatemaltecas are formulating a counterdiscourse that rejects separating production from social reproduction and privileging economics over culture while appreciating local agencies. One should not expect, however, that this resistance will go unchallenged, either internally or externally to the movement. The Central American Free Trade Agreement will surely set the stage for a new set of negotiations—between Guatemaltecas and between women and Others.

LEARNING FROM THE GUATEMALAN CASE

What can be learned from the experiences of the Guatemalan women's movement? For one thing, the case solicits the need for a reexamination of social movements under global restructuring. Specifically, it calls into question a core assumption of new social movement theory: that movement mobilization will inevitably strengthen civil society. It shows instead how social movements are embedded within local, national, and international power constructs that limit the form and content of the movements. State-directed political and economic reforms after 1986 in Guatemala, for example, did open political spaces to women, but they also restricted the mobilization of the women's movement by setting the parameters of organization, dialogues, and policies about gender.

This study also illustrates the ways in which civil society is "mined by unequal relations of power."[34] This leads to the privileging of some discourses over others and to the representation of some women but not others. Due largely to power differentials, the Guatemalan women's movement came to speak well for some women—urban and mestiza women—while ignoring or only peripherally representing others—rural and indigenous women. When activists attempted to bridge power differentials to strengthen the women's movement, they often found it difficult to organize across the intersecting ethnic and class lines. As a result, the Guatemalan women's movement at times barely resembled a movement at all, but in reality was a group of separate organizations pursuing distinct goals with little or no contact with each other.

Globalization may, however, slowly be providing some of the conditions under which links can be made to better connect women's movements internally. It is forcing changes in the roles women play in the economic and political spheres. As a consequence, women are being brought together not just physically, across traditional boundaries of class, ethnicity, and sexuality, but are being encouraged to build strategic alliances around gender. Though not necessarily severing ties with mixed-gender class, ethnic, or gay groups, Guatemalan women, for example, have begun to explore ways to create women's "unity with diversity." Akin to the strategic feminist formulations of Mohanty discussed in the first chapter, Guatemaltecas have begun to try to build strategic bridges between themselves around diverse definitions of gender rights. In doing so, they are constructing women's and female identity as the right to have intimate relations with whomever one wants, the right to wear traditional Maya clothes, the right to have or not have children, the right to work, the right to participate in political activities, and the like. Quite simply, Guatemaltecas are building a strategic identity founded on rights rather than on needs or interests.

Additionally, the study demonstrates the inherent instability of gender construction within the globalization project as well as the malleability of patriarchy. Global restructuring at once depends on traditional gender constructions but also requires the liberalization of gender norms and a reconfiguration of the patriarchy. In the factory, for instance, the factory owner relies on the availability of cheap, malleable female labor. Women are thus encouraged to break with conventional gender norms to enter the formal economy, but once on the factory floor, they are required to submit to traditional gendered inequities. One would predict that it will be difficult for capitalistic interests to sustain these contradictions for an extended period of time. Still, the Guatemalan case has illustrated the malleability of patriarchy and the multiple and astute ways in which the state has helped to maneuver the gender minefield in support of global capital. There is no certainty as to the outcome; the story continues to be constructed.

NOTES

CHAPTER 1. FACE-OFF: GENDER, DEMOCRATIZATION, AND GLOBALIZATION

1. "In addition to questioning the social institutions, the different feminist currents are confronting the global and local spaces within which we develop." Velásquez Nimatuj, "Desigualdades," 10.

2. I use "North/northern" to refer to so-called advanced or developed countries and "South/southern" to denote so-called Third World or developing countries. I have done so in an attempt to employ less value-charged terms, even though I realize they, too, are problematic.

3. For a fuller discussion of the relationship between the women's movement and politics, see Jaquette, *Women's Movement in Latin America*.

4. Slater, "Rethinking," 385.

5. Cohen and Arato, *Civil Society*, 518.

6. Pepper, *Eco-Socialism*, 137.

7. Slater, "Rethinking," 388.

8. Alvarez, Dagnino, and Escobar, "Latin American Social Movements," 18.

9. Marchand and Runyan, "Introduction," 14.

10. Bayes, Hawkesworth, and Kelly, "Globalization," 3.

11. Waylen, "Gender," 7. Though Waylen in this quote is offering a feminist reconceptualization of the state, not a neoliberal definition, I argue that the "feminist" modifications are joining with neoliberal definitions.

12. Schild, " 'Gender Equity,' " 26.

13. Schild, "Neo-liberalism's New Gendered Citizens," 277.

14. Ibid., 278.

15. Marchand and Runyan, "Introduction," 18.

16. Ibid.

17. Schild, "Neo-liberalism's New Gendered Citizens," 277–278.

18. Marchand and Runyan, "Introduction," 18.

19. Bayes, Hawkesworth, and Kelly, "Globalization," 4.

20. Schild, "New Subjects of Rights?" 99.

21. Yúdice, "New Civil Society," 363.

22. Sonia Alvarez, "Advocating Feminism."

23. Yúdice, "New Civil Society," 373.

24. Ibid., 358.

25. Mohanty, *Feminism without Borders*, 235.

26. Marchand and Runyan, "Introduction," 12.

27. "Ripe for Rape," *The Economist*, January 15, 1994, 65. Quoted in Hooper, "Masculinities in Transition," 68-69.

28. Ibid., 69.

29. Stephen, *Women and Social Movements*, 20.

30. Ibid., 21.

31. Ibid.

32. Molyneux, "Analyzing Women's Movements," 235.

33. Wiernga, "Women's Interests and Empowerment," 829-848.

34. Rai, *Political Economy of Development*, 163-168; Molyneux, "Analyzing Women's Movements," 231-242.

35. Stephen, "Past Trends and New Directions," 83.

36. Jonasdottir, "On the Concept of Interests," 33-65.

37. Rai, *Political Economy of Development*, 165.

38. Spivak, "Can the Subaltern Speak?" 271-313.

39. Batliwala, "Women's Empowerment," 130.

40. Kabeer, "Conflicts over Credit," 81.

41. Molyneux, "Analyzing Women's Movements," 227.

42. Ibid.

43. Martin, "Extraordinary Homosexuals," 111.

44. Franco, *Plotting Women*, xi.

45. Sanford, "From I, Rigoberta," 29. Sanford uses the figures of the Commission for Historical Clarification (Comisión para el Esclarecimiento Histórico; CEH) published in its 1999 study, *Guatemala: Memory of Silence* (Guatemala City: CEH).

46. Stephen, "Anthropological Research," 83.

47. Cathy Blacklock argues that "the national security strategy pursued by the military through the early 1980s had as its longer-term objective the political liberalization of Guatemala" (2). Although the military did have modernization goals, most importantly the restructuring of rural production, I disagree slightly with the impression that Blacklock gives that political liberalization was one of the military's main objectives. Instead, I contend that the military decided to return power to a civilian government in the mid-1980s, not because it was part of its modernization project, but only in response to the augmentation of organized popular resistance, international pressures, and the dissatisfaction of the national business elite over economic policies and performance. Blacklock, "Democratization," 1-12.

48. The Puebla-Panama Plan and Central American Free Trade Agreement (CAFTA) seek to open up southern Mexico and Central America to private foreign investment and set the stage for the foundation for the Free Trade Area of the Americas. The Puebla-Panama Plan would channel some $10 billion of for-

eign aid and local tax dollars to build the infrastructure—including hydroelectric plants, seaports, highways, railroads, and more—for industrialization in the region. Meanwhile, CAFTA would take steps to establish regional free trade and lay the groundwork for the eventual creation of the Free Trade Area of the Americas.

49. As late as 1997, Eugenia Mijangos wrote in an article in *Debate* that Guatemalan women involved in various organizations were still debating whether or not there *was* a "women's movement" in Guatemala. Mijangos, "La organización de género," 29.

50. Schild, "New Subjects of Rights?" 95.

51. In Guatemala, "*maquila(s)*" is the term used for *maquiladora(s)*.

CHAPTER 2. INSIDE (AND) OUT: HOME, WORK, AND ORGANIZING

1. "You don't hear them / but they listen. / They are sitting in the back. / When finally they raise a hand, / they unveil their face / of a word / with eyes of a scared hare / that flees from the kitchens / from the rooms / and the living rooms / to peek / —even if it is for only an instant—/ in a place without walls / but with a soul." Escobar Sarti, "Women You Don't Hear," 49. The translation above from Spanish to English is by Vivian Rivas.

2. Francisca Ixcaptá led an attack against Spanish colonial officials in her village, Santa Catarina Iztahuacán, in 1814, was captured and imprisoned, only to escape and lead another attack on the prison. Dolores Bedoya de Molina (1783–1853) encouraged women to participate in the anticolonial struggle and after independence, involved herself in Liberal politics. Monzón, "Rasgos históricos," 5–8.

3. Vicente Lapara de la Cerda (1831–1905) edited an early women's newspaper, *La Voz de la Mujer*. María Josefa García Granados scandalized Guatemalan society at the turn of the twentieth century with her political satire and independent ways—going to Europe alone, attending literary gatherings with men, and walking unaccompanied on Guatemalan streets. Monzón, "Rasgos históricos," 7.

4. Women's participation in the overthrow of dictator Jorge Ubico and in building a new democratic society during the reform years from 1944 to 1954 has too long been neglected. Norma Stoltz Chinchilla helps to rescue and preserve some of the history of women during this period in *Nuestras utopías: Mujeres guatemaltecas del siglo xx* (1998). Through the testimonies of women from different class, cultural, and political backgrounds, the book details women's active participation but also the political, family, and economic restraints placed on them during this time. The Alianza Femenina de Guatemala (Guatemalan Women's Alliance) is a case in point. Formed by political wives of the 1944-1954 years, the Alianza sought to politicize women both around gender issues and in support of the revolutionary reforms. The organization received a small monthly subsidy from the government, and in general its goals coalesced with those of the gov-

ernment. Thus they encouraged women to use their new power to vote—granted in the 1945 Constitution—and visited farms so that "while the men got together to discuss labor issues, we got together the women. We explained to them the Agrarian Reform [passed by the Arbenz government in 1952], and the ways in which, along with their husbands, they could apply for land or work in agriculture. We also talked with them about how their husbands treated them" (Stoltz Chinchilla, *Nuestras utopias*, 54). In another case, when a woman, Hortensia Hernández Rojas, was proposed as the secretary general of the Confederación de Trabajadores de Guatemala (Confederation of Guatemalan Workers; CTG), the main labor federation, her name was withdrawn from candidacy after male unionists expressed "shame" at the possibility of having a female union president. Nevertheless, Hernández Rojas became the leader of the Unión Social de Trabajadores de Hechura y Confección de Ropa (Social Union of Clothing Cutters and Assembly Workers) and was appointed secretary of finances of the CTG (Monzón, "Rasgos históricos," 16–19).

5. The nineteenth-century debate over the definition of citizenship ultimately excluded those who were illiterate—and, consequently, the majority of the indigenous population (except those who owned property valued at more than Q1,000 or were artisans in recognized municipal workshops)—and women from political rights. It was argued that because women were "destined to be mothers, they should not allow themselves to worry about public matters" and that men would better represent them in the public sphere (Monzón, "Rasgos históricos," 21). Thus, while all women were disenfranchised, indigenous women were excluded twice over: by their ethnicity and by their gender. Like women, indigenous citizens did not obtain the right to vote until 1945.

6. For example, Aurora Morales, the daughter of merchants in Guatemala City, says, "When I got to sixth grade my father told me that my studies would end there. I wanted to continue, especially to get out of the house because I really did not like staying home. But my father asked why? 'When you are married, are you going to wrap your children up in your diploma? Are you going to put the diploma on the plate of your husband? You don't need to study, you'll learn bad habits (and) make inappropriate friends'" (Stoltz Chinchilla, *Nuestras utopias*, 23). Earlier, Aurora Morales notes, "My father was a very intelligent man, but my mother was a merchant." The text sheds light not only on historical gender inequities but also on their internalization. It is interesting that she feels the need to point out that her father was intelligent just before discussing her mother's commercial success. The sentence structure implies that possibly one cannot be intelligent and "muy comerciante" or that intelligence is gendered (Stoltz Chinchilla, *Nuestras utopias*, 19).

7. Aurora Morales notes that during the early twentieth century it was still customary for sisters to serve their brothers; sisters washed their brothers' clothes and dishes, mended and sewed their clothes, etc. (Stoltz Chinchilla, *Nuestras utopias*, 22). Aura Marina Arriola, the daughter of a diplomat during the 1944–

1954 years, says of her father, "He believed a woman was in need of support, of protection." Further, when asked why he did not go to church, he argued that the church was there to support women (88). See also the *Código Civil* (1877).

8. Monzón, "Rasgos históricos," 9.

9. Ibid.

10. Sanborn, "Travels in Guatemala," 162.

11. This was happening not just in Guatemala, but comparable events were occurring throughout Latin America. See studies such as Jane S. Jaquette's *Women's Movement in Latin America* (1991); Lynn Stephen's *Women and Social Movements in Latin America* (1997); Elizabeth Dore's *Gender Politics in Latin America* (1997); and Sonia Alvarez' *Engendering Democracy in Brazil* (1990).

12. Blacklock, "Popular Women's Political Organizations," 5.

13. Ibid.

14. The Guatemalan left-wing insurgent movement had its roots in a coup by young military officers in the early 1960s. The coup failed, but a new political force was born. The officer corps refused to punish the conspirators, and two of their leaders, Luis Turcios Lima and Marco Antonio Yon Sosa, both second lieutenants, went into a brief, self-imposed exile. When they returned, they tried to unify the opposition behind a program of democratic and social reforms but ultimately concluded that such an alliance was not viable. On 6 February 1962, Yon Sosa formed the first guerrilla front, and in March 1962, the Communist Party formed its own guerrilla front under the leadership of Carlos Paz Tejada. Over the next two decades, these organizations formed coalitions, split, and redefined themselves. Still, none of them gained real popular support until the late 1970s. Indeed, between 1962 and 1978 the combined membership of the various fronts was at most 6,000 and at times was much less. In January 1982, several independent guerrilla fronts united to form the URNG. Black, *Garrison Guatemala*, 84.

15. Using scorched-earth techniques, the military destroyed rural villages and then forced survivors to move into "model villages" or "strategic hamlets." These villages were completely controlled by the military: residents had to get permission to leave the towns, entrance into the villages was restricted, and the use of native languages and the practice of non-Christian religions was forbidden.

16. The military government created the civil patrol system in 1982 and rapidly expanded it throughout the countryside. All village men over fifteen years of age were required to "volunteer" time to help guard their town from "subversives." Though purportedly voluntary, participation was in reality compulsory, since anyone who failed to "volunteer" was suspected of having subversive tendencies and had to face the consequences of being so labeled. The civil patrol system became an important tool of the military to control rural populations.

17. Sieder et al., *Who Governs?*, 1.

18. Rising state repression affected family relations in a variety of obvious and not so obvious ways. Calel, for instance, initially blamed her husband for the fact that she had to discard the indigenous feminine garb. "When my husband fell for

the first time in the hands of the military. First, I cut my hair and seeing myself in the mirror I began to cry. I fought a lot with my husband; I told him it was his fault that I had to cut my hair. The second time that the military grabbed him, my *compañeros* had a serious talk with me. They told me that if I did not stop wearing the indigenous *traje*, we would be more easily spotted in the capital . . . Seeing the risk that we ran, not only for ourselves but for many other *compañeros* of the organization [CUC], I stopped wearing the *traje* . . . When we stopped using the indigenous *traje*, we would run into people we knew in Quiché. They would laugh at us. I would hide my face in shame." Stoltz Chinchilla, *Nuestras utopias*, 323–324.

19. In the mid-1980s, a Guatemalan factory owner expressed this supremely racist viewpoint to me. He contended that the Americans had ultimately done the right thing in decimating the northern indigenous populations early in their country's history because in doing so, he argued, they had gotten rid of a major roadblock to capitalist development. Guatemala, in contrast, he lamented, had been more humane and had not destroyed the "backward" and recalcitrant indigenous cultures. It was to this that he attributed Guatemala's delayed development.

20. Linda Green, in *Fear as a Way of Life* (1999), traces changes in gender roles and relations in rural Guatemala with the expansion of capitalism in the 1940s–1960s.

21. *Guatemala: La fuerza incluyente del desarrollo humano.*

22. Deere and León, *Mujer y tierra en Guatemala*, 6–9.

23. Prior to Vatican II, the Catholic Church encouraged the formation of hierarchical sociopolitical organizations in Guatemala to vigorously propagate religious and social values in the larger society. These Catholic Action programs focused on leadership training, creating labor unions, and establishing political parties. After Vatican II, Catholic Action slowly gave way to the growth of Christian Base Communities, or CEBs, which were small community organizations made up of lay people who, using the Bible as a guide, sought to promote socioeconomic and political reforms in their communities.

24. Smith-Ayala, *Granddaughters of Ixmucané*, 59–60.

25. Though these organizations might generally be considered practical or materialist according to feminist categories, they were also rights based. The concept of rights has proven to be a key organizing tool and unifying point for the Guatemalan women's movement.

26. See Schirmer, " 'Those Who Die,' " 41–76.

27. For a discussion of the formation and early years of CUC, see Rigoberta Menchú, *Rigoberta: La nieta de los mayas* (1998).

28. Smith-Ayala, *Granddaughters of Ixmucané*; Hooks, *Guatemalan Women Speak*; Harbury, *Bridge of Courage*.

29. Jelin, "Engendering Human Rights," 77.

30. Stoltz Chinchilla, *Nuestras utopias*, 275.

31. Ibid., 312–313.

32. Ibid., 310.

33. For example, Margarita, who became active in community development projects through Catholic Action, slowly came to the conclusion that she really didn't need to teach women about nutrition and health care—they already knew how to feed and care for their children—they just did not have the money to buy what was needed. She consequently began to organize women to make their demands, not only on the state, but also on their husbands and families. Stoltz Chinchilla, *Nuestras utopias*, 278–279.

34. The play between politics and gender is interesting in this quote. Communism is subtly linked to loose morals, to *bad* women, and to *bad* men who take advantage of *good* women. Stoltz Chinchilla, *Nuestras utopias*, 287.

35. Aron et al., "Gender-Specific Terror," 37–47.

36. For instance, Elena Tecún remembers her anger when she witnessed members of the army stripping a woman of her clothes in the middle of the day in a Quiché market; they then "sent her home" without anything to wear. Stoltz Chinchilla, *Nuestras utopias*, 390.

37. Yolanda Aguilar, quoted in Stoltz Chinchilla, *Nuestras utopias*, 368–369.

38. Aura Marina Azucena Bolaños, quoted in Stoltz Chinchilla, *Nuestras utopias*, 191.

39. Harbury, *Bridge of Courage*, 152.

40. It would be easy to blame the slowness of social movements in highlighting gender on their agendas to the male dominance of many organizations. However, female-led organizations also subordinated gender to class. Although largely female led, GAM went through this kind of process. Initially gender was not on the agenda whatsoever, and members only slowly accepted its inclusion after the organization was repeatedly confronted by the brutal rape tactics of the armed forces. Thus, no matter who led the organizations, early social movements were dominated by the institutionalization of patriarchal notions that subordinated gender to class and ethnic concerns. Still, from the beginning, women participating in these very different kinds of organizations lobbied for gendered changes, or as the URNG recruit put it, "We never accepted that."

41. Smith-Ayala, *Granddaughters of Ixmucané*, 212.

42. Harbury, *Bridge of Courage*. See also Colom, *Mujeres en la alborada* (1998).

43. Smith-Ayala, *Granddaughters of Ixmucané*, 77.

44. Schild, "New Subjects of Rights," 113.

45. The neoliberal focus was demonstrated by the types of loan agreements reached between the Guatemalan government and international funding agencies such as the Inter-American Bank and the World Bank. For more discussion, see Ruthrauff and Carlson, *Inter-American Development Bank* (1997).

46. Jaquette, *Women's Movement in Latin America*, 13.

47. Pellecer, interview with the author, 19 May 1998; Pellecer and Ponce, interview with the author, 27 November 2002.

48. Lemus, interview with the author, 20 May 1998.

49. Ibid.

50. This shift was occurring not only in Guatemala but also throughout the rest of Latin America. Explanations for the conservative trend vary but include the ideological preferences and anticommunist beliefs of the new pope, Pope John Paul II, inaugurated in 1978; fear of rising strife within the church between the left and the right; the intensification of public questioning of church hierarchal structures of power; the weakening of elite support for the Catholic Church; and the rise of Protestant evangelicalism in Latin America.

51. Guatemalteca organizations consistently note "*capacitación*" as one of their projects. I have decided to rather awkwardly translate *capacitación* as "capacity training," by which I hope to maintain a feeling from the original of power inequity between the enabler and the enabled: women's organizations are seeking to enable other women, their clients. This *capacitación* project requires the transfer of some fairly intangible capabilities that will empower the client. As such, it is a relationship founded in, but seeking to surpass, inequity.

52. Rivas, interviews with the author, 22 May 1998 and 28 November 2002.

53. Female labor unionists are up against enormous odds in Guatemala. Not only is there a long tradition of state and employer repression against unionization, but the women who *do* become union leaders and embrace a gendered analysis often face difficulties from their husbands at home. As Olga Rivas noted, activists often end up losing both their jobs and their husbands, becoming single mothers. So the costs of organizing can be enormous for women. Rivas, interviews with the author, 22 May 1998 and 28 November 2002.

54. Schirmer, "Seeking of Truth," 52.

55. The Catholic Church's continued support for CONAVIGUA was partially due to its close historical relationship with the organization during the repressive era, but also to the fact that CONAVIGUA never labeled itself as feminist or institutionally questioned the church's mandates on social reproduction.

56. The Convergencia Cívico Política de Mujeres (Women's Civic Political Convergence; CCPM) was formed in 1994 to "encourage the involvement of women from various ideological perspectives, life and work experiences, skills and residences, in existing socio-political organizations or that such organizations be formed that meet the specific demands of women." Tierra Viva, *Poder, liderazgo y participación política*, 17.

57. For more discussion on the role of NGOs in development, see Fisher, *Nongovernments* (1998).

58. I made this observation based on multiple interviews I conducted with women activists in Guatemala between 1998 and 2003.

59. Armas España, interview with the author, 19 May 1998; Rodríguez, interview with the author, 19 May 1998.

60. Armas España, interview with the author, 19 May 1998.

61. Sector de Mujeres, *Mujeres construyendo la paz*, 3.

62. Ibid., 1.

63. Oficina Nacional de la Mujer and Proyecto Mujer y Reformas Jurídicas, *Obligaciones legislativas*, 16.

64. MacNabb, "Guatemalan Women," 201–231.

65. SEPAZ and the women negotiators initially agreed to form a thirteen-member Coordinating Commission to design, promote, and organize the Foro. At the last minute, the government decided to appoint only a ten-member commission, arguing that civil society was overrepresented. The ten-member Commission consisted of six representatives from civil society and four from the government and began operating on 21 May 1997. The last-minute reduction maneuverings of the government served to oust representatives from feminist organizations.

66. MacNabb, "Guatemalan Women," 201–231; Marroquín, "Cumplimiento de los acuerdos," 9.

67. MacNabb, "Guatemalan Women," 201–231.

68. Many thought that ONAM should have been put in charge of designing a public policy on women, since it was the existing state agency set up to coordinate state policies on women.

69. Sector de Mujeres, *Caminando hacia la institucionalización*, 14–15.

70. Ibid.

71. Sandra Morán, interview with the author, 18 May 1998.

72. Ibid.

CHAPTER 3. *La goma elástica:* CODIFYING AND
INSTITUTIONALIZING WOMEN IN POSTWAR GUATEMALA

1. "The peace accords recognize the necessity that the woman widely participate in the construction of democracy in Guatemala and freely exercise her civil and political rights. In order to accomplish this, it is necessary to overcome discrimination" (MINUGUA, *Los desafíos*, n.p.).

2. In a conversation with Carol Cohn published in *Signs* in 2003, Enloe endorses the use of the term *patriarchy* despite the misgivings of some. She says, "*Patriarchy* is not a sledge-hammer being swung around a raving feminist head. It is a tool; it sheds light at the same time as it reveals patterns of causality. . . . It means you have to ask about the daily operations of both masculinity and femininity in relationship to each. It is not men-on-top that makes something patriarchal. It's men who are recognized and claim a certain form of masculinity, for the sake of being more valued, more 'serious,' and 'the protectors of and controllers of those people who are less masculine' that makes any organization, any community, any society patriarchal" (Carol Cohn and Cynthia Enloe, "Conversation," 1192).

3. Marshall, *Citizenship and Social Class* (1950).

4. Fallon, "Women's Citizenship Rights," 525–543. See also Basu, *Local Feminisms* (1995); Craske, *Women and Politics* (1999); and Jelin, *Women and Social Change* (1990).

5. Puwar, "Interview with Carole Pateman," 130–132.

6. Carole Pateman warns feminists against the allure of contracts (be it marriage, employment, or political), arguing that institutions are gendered and power is distributed unequally: "Powers are structurally there in the institutions so . . . when you make the change from 'man' to 'husband' you acquire the powers, which you use or not. But the point is that you have the powers by virtue of the contract that has been entered into and the structure of the institution of which you are now a part" (ibid., 127).

7. Enloe, "Demilitarization," 29.

8. Ibid., 24.

9. The discussion of exceptions for women in the Guatemalan Constitution is almost always followed by exceptions for blind and handicapped and minors (e.g., Article 102). The *Ley para prevenir, sancionar y erradicar la violencia intrafamiliar* passed in 1996 also makes this inappropriate link between women and individuals who, because of age or disability, are dependent on healthy male adults. It states that the law "especially protects women, children, young people, the elderly and disabled." Guatemala, *Código Civil* (1963), *Ley para prevenir, sancionar y erradicar la violencia intrafamiliar (Decreto 97–96)*, Article 2.

10. Squires, *Gender in Political Theory*, 118–121.

11. Ibid., 118–119.

12. Oficina Nacional de la Mujer and Proyecto Mujer y Reformas Jurídicas, *Obligaciones legislativas*, 12–13, 44, 96.

13. Ibid., 14.

14. Oficina Nacional de la Mujer and Proyecto Mujer y Reformas Jurídicas, "Acuerdo sobre Identidad y Derechos de los Pueblos Indígenas," Section II, Part B, #1, in *Obligaciones legislativas*, 31–32.

15. Ibid.

16. Ibid., 32.

17. García Montenegro, interview with the author, 22 May 1998.

18. Waylen, "Gender," 1.

19. Ibid., 8.

20. Del Cid Vargas, "Estrategias," 3.

21. As stated in the original *Ley para prevenir, sancionar y erradicar la violencia intrafamiliar*, Article 1 does not gender violence as the interpretation quoted here does. Majawil Q'ij, Ukux Ulew, Defensoría de la Mujer Maya, Asociación de Mujeres Nuevo Amanecer, *Decreto Gubernativo 97–96*, 5.

22. Comisión de la Mujer, el Menor y la Familia, *Conociendo la ley*.

23. Some women's groups expressed dissatisfaction with the way the women's program of the Centro para Acción Legal en Derechos Humanos (CALDH) dominated COALM. Alarcón Alba, *Diagnostic Study*, n.p.

24. COALM received initial technical and methodological support from the Washington Office on Latin America (ibid.).

25. Guatemala, *Código Civil* (1963), Articles 113 and 114.

26. Neocitizens are individualistic, self-motivated, and self-sufficient, and thus neither need nor seek socioeconomic assistance from the state.

27. Protest from the Catholic Church centered on Articles 6, 25, 26, 29, and 31, which recognized nonmarried couples and single-headed households as families, supported the use of family planning methods, and mandated the formation of a sex education curriculum in the schools. Guatemala, *Código Civil* (1963), *Ley de desarrollo social*, 2–3, 7–10.

28. According to the Grupo Interagencial de Género y Adelanto de la Mujer (Interagency Group on Gender and Women's Advancement; GIGAM), approximately four out of every ten homes in Guatemala is headed by a woman, and 71.8 percent of those homes live in extreme poverty. About 21 percent depend upon the work of their children to help provide the family with subsistence. MINUGUA, "Mirada a los compromisos," 2.

29. Guatemala, *Código Civil* (1963), *Ley de desarrollo social*, Article 10.

30. Ibid., Article 15.

31. The debate centered on the use of contraceptives and on sex education. While women's groups supported the use of chemical contraceptives and the provision of sex education in public schools, the Catholic Church supported only natural methods of contraception and favored the family as the primary vehicle for disseminating information about sexuality and reproduction. Mercedes Arzú, president of the Family Foundation of the Americas, claimed that "the approval of the laws containing any such compromises in state education represents a conspiracy by international actors, including the UN and the US, to force foreign values on Guatemala" ("Sex Education Debate," 2).

32. Asturias, "Guatemala: Aprueban Ley de desarrollo social," 3.

33. *Constitución Política de la República de Guatemala*, 47–48.

34. The Women in Development (WID) approach demanded the integration of women into the development process. WID supporters contended that the exclusion of women from development policymaking and implementation had not only resulted in hardships for Third World women but had also led to the creation of faulty development projects. It thus recommended cooperative development with the participation of women. By the 1990s, however, some women involved with development had turned away from WID cooperation to embrace another approach, Gender and Development (GAD). GAD supporters stressed the unequal gender relations and power inequities of inappropriate development policies and called for the empowerment of all women as the only way to ultimately improve conditions for poor women. (See also Chap. 6, n. 29.)

35. It must be remembered that 60 percent of the Guatemalan female population is illiterate, and the Human Rights Ombudsman's office estimates that between 75 percent and 90 percent of all indigenous women are illiterate.

36. "Presidente convocó," sec. A.

37. Sector de Mujeres, *Caminando hacia la institucionalización* and *Ejerciendo nuestra ciudadanía,* 7-32.

38. MINUGUA, "Interview with Lili Caravantes," 4.

39. According to Caravantes, international funding does not sustain SEPREM but does help it to achieve its goals. Lili Caravantes, interview with the author, 26 November 2002.

40. The conflicting roles Caravantes must play—state bureaucrat and women's advocate—were clearly evident in an interview with the author in November 2002. For example, when asked about the origins of SEPREM, Caravantes stated that the women's movement had lobbied the Guatemalan government to form SEPREM. Although it is true that the women's movement had pressured for the creation of an autonomous women's agency, activists had not visualized an organ like SEPREM and did not generally support its creation. Later in the same interview, Caravantes admitted to some difficulties and strained relations between SEPREM, some women's groups, and already existing government agencies such as ONAM and Foro. Caravantes, interview with the author, 26 November 2002.

41. Ibid.

42. Ibid.

43. Ibid.

44. Upon his inauguration in 2004, President Oscar Berger appointed sociologist María Gabriela Núñez Pérez to replace Caravantes as head of SEPREM.

45. The labor code effectively excludes domestic employees from basic labor rights, particularly the right to an eight-hour workday and a forty-eight-hour workweek. They are also generally denied employee health care and the minimum wage. The proposed law would rectify some of these inequities. For a discussion of the working conditions of domestic workers in Guatemala, see Human Rights Watch, *From the Household to the Factory,* 63-109.

CHAPTER 4. *T* IS FOR *Tortillera?* SEXUAL MINORITIES AND IDENTITY POLITICS

1. Gaspar de Alba, "Descarada/No Shame," in *The Wild Good,* 217-223, and reprinted in Gaspar de Alba, *La Llorona on the Longfellow Bridge,* 90. The lines were translated and quoted on the back cover of the *Identidades: Lesbianas guatemaltecas en su diversidad* 1, no. 00 (July 2000).

2. López Sologaistoa, interview with the author, 28 November 2002.

3. Ibid.

4. Simo, "Guatemala: Making an Oasis."

5. D'Emilio, "Capitalism and Gay Identity," 169-178.

6. Stein, "Sisters and Queers," 378-391; McClure, "Sexuality, Power, and Performance," 311.

7. McClure, "Sexuality, Power, and Performance," 11-12.

8. Morris, "Educating Desire," 39.

9. Altman, "Rupture or Continuity?" 91.

10. McClure, "Sexuality, Power, and Performance," 21.

11. Altman, "Rupture or Continuity?" 77.

12. Norma Mogrovejo is one of the most well-known "*lesbianólogas*" in Mexico. Peruvian by birth, she has lived in Mexico since 1987. She is the founder of the Archivo Histórico Lésbico Nancy Cárdenas in Mexico City and the author of numerous books and articles on the lesbian movement in Latin America. Mogrovejo, "Sexual Preferences," 324.

13. Ibid., 311.

14. Some lesbians disagreed and questioned the relevance for the majority of lesbians of the feminist focus on reproduction rights. Ibid., 311–312.

15. Ibid., 316–317.

16. Ibid., 317.

17. Ibid.

18. Ibid., 323.

19. Stein, "Sisters and Queers," 380.

20. The 1969 police raid on a New York City gay bar, the Stonewall Bar, and the defiant response by bar patrons, has become an international symbol of the start of the gay rights movement.

21. It must be kept in mind that, to date, no major, sustained study has yet documented the emergence, history, or formation of alternative articulations of sexuality within recent Guatemalan history. Hence, those movements that stand in opposition to or simply in proximity to those addressed in this chapter await further research.

22. Altman, "Rupture or Continuity?" 85.

23. Murray, *Latin American Male Homosexualities*, 75.

24. McClure, "Sexuality, Power, and Performance," 139.

25. López Sologaistoa, interview with the author, 28 November 2002.

26. Ibid.

27. Pile, "Introduction," 28.

28. Acevedo and Sams, "Editorial," 3.

29. McClure, "Sexuality, Power, and Performance," 316.

30. Altman, "Rupture or Continuity?" 81.

31. Rummel, *Saliendo del closet*, 6.

32. Ibid., 15; 14; 22; 23.

33. Ibid., 41–42; 25.

34. Anonymous interview with the author in Guatemala City, 27 November 2002.

35. This becomes clear in reading Rummel, *Saliendo del closet*.

36. Arlene Stein argues that prior to Stonewall, women in the United States who joined lesbian groups also "were more likely to be of working-class origin,

due at least in part to the fact that they tended to be less concerned with losing social status. Women encouraged to 'elect' lesbianism through exposure to feminism, by contrast, were more likely to come from the middle class" ("Sisters and Queers," 384).

37. Calderón, "How to Be a Lesbian in Guatemala."

38. McClure, "Sexuality, Power, and Performance," 329.

39. Acevedo, interview with the author, 27 November 2002.

40. Jorge López Sologaistoa confirmed the importance of national and international events to the formation of OASIS, saying, "After the peace process began in the region, we have had more opportunities to live more openly and to demand respect. The international community has played a very important role, as it has supported us in this process." López Sologaistoa, quoted in Stern, "Gay Life Emerges."

41. McClure, "Sexuality, Power, and Performance," 185–186.

42. Rummel, *Saliendo del closet*, 15.

43. Acevedo, cited in Calderón, "How to Be a Lesbian in Guatemala."

44. Ibid.

45. López Sologaistoa, interview with the author, 28 November 2002.

46. Violence against gays in Guatemala is high. In fact, a couple of months after my interview with Jorge López Sologaistoa, unknown men tried unsuccessfully to abduct him at gunpoint. Moreover, victims of violence are often labeled gay after their attack in an attempt to minimize the public's sympathy for the victim. Such rumors circulated, for instance, after the deaths of Myrna Mack, Dianna Ortiz, and Bishop Juan Gerardi—all victims of the Guatemalan security forces.

47. Sams, "Lesbian Liberation," 8.

48. López Sologaistoa joked that "Mujer-es Somos (We Are Women) became Mujeres Fuimos (We Women Left)." López Sologaistoa, interview with the author, 28 November 2002.

49. López Sologaistoa told me that despite animosity between the two groups, OASIS helped Lesbiradas financially make the move (ibid.).

50. Acevedo, interview with the author, 27 November 2002; López Sologaistoa, interview with the author, 28 November 2002.

51. Dagnino, "Citizenship in Latin America," 4.

52. Rummel, *Saliendo del closet*, 21.

53. Ibid., 48.

54. Ibid.

55. Acevedo, cited in Calderón, "How to Be a Lesbian in Guatemala."

56. Rummel, *Saliendo del closet*, 69.

57. Heather McClure argues that lesbians might have assumed that feminists and the larger women's movement would be unwelcoming of lesbian needs and they thus never openly approached the organizations. So although she acknowledges that the women's movement was exclusionary in some ways, she also main-

tains that preconceived prejudices or fears on the part of lesbians might also have kept the two groups apart ("Sexuality, Power, and Performance," 320).

58. Ibid., 322.

59. I conclude this from interviews with the leaders of women's organizations in Guatemala in November 2002.

60. Acevedo, interview with the author, 27 November 2002.

61. Sams, "Lesbian Liberation," 8.

CHAPTER 5. THE "SWALLOW INDUSTRIES": FLIGHT, CONSUMPTION, AND INDIGESTION

1. Factory worker Mercedes Barrios told Deborah Levenson-Estrada in January 1991 that the unionized women at ACRICASA would taunt men at nearby factories with "We are women and we've organized . . . what have you men done?" In this way, they questioned both the men's class leadership but also their masculinity. Levenson-Estrada, "Working-Class Feminism," 214.

2. In a survey of forty female *maquila* workers in 1992, the Asociación para el Avance de las Ciencias Sociales en Guatemala (Association for the Advancement of Social Sciences in Guatemala; AVANCSO) found that twenty-two had not previously worked outside the home, ten had at one time been domestic workers, three had worked in commercial enterprises, and only five had previously worked in a factory. AVANCSO, *El significado de la maquila,* 71.

3. Mattson, "Maquila in Guatemala."

4. Human Rights Watch, *From the Household to the Factory,* 3; VESTEX, "Guatemala Apparel and Textile Industry."

5. Petersen, *Maquiladora Revolution,* 197.

6. Mattson, "Maquila in Guatemala."

7. AVANCSO, *El significado de la maquila,* 21-24.

8. USAID and international and domestic Guatemalan elites argued that Guatemala could develop economically without land reform or other redistributive policies but with the increased exportation of nontraditional products. Petersen, *Maquiladora Revolution,* 14.

9. Ibid., 30.

10. Human Rights Watch, *From the Household to the Factory,* 57; VESTEX, "Apparel Exports to the United States."

11. AVANCSO, *El significado de la maquila,* 32-34.

12. Human Rights Watch, *From the Household to the Factory,* 57-58.

13. Petersen, *Maquiladora Revolution,* 26; United States Agency for International Development (hereafter USAID), "Guatemala."

14. Petersen, *Maquiladora Revolution,* 27.

15. USAID, "Guatemala"; Human Rights Watch, *From the Household to the Factory,* 57; Petersen, *Maquiladora Revolution,* 27.

16. Petersen, *Maquiladora Revolution,* 16.

17. Ibid., 17.

18. FUNDESA, *Business Guidebook*. Also see Petersen, *Maquiladora Revolution*, 18.

19. It is difficult to verify the number of operating *maquilas* at any given time. In fact, the numbers cited here differ from those reported by Human Rights Watch in January 2002. Human Rights Watch listed 255 existing *maquilas*, of which 145 were Korean owned, 77 Guatemalan owned, 18 U.S. owned, and 11 owned by individuals from a variety of other countries. Human Rights Watch, *From the Household to the Factory*, 55. The VESTEX statistics cited here are from VESTEX, "Investment Capital." Also see AVANCSO, *El significado de la maquila*, xv.

20. Petersen, *Maquiladora Revolution*, 145.

21. According to AVANCSO, the first South Korean *maquila* was established in 1984. The number of South Korean–financed factories remained small, however, until 1988 and 1989. In 1987, there were eight South Korean *maquilas;* in 1988, that number rose to fifteen; in 1989, there were thirty-seven; and in 1990, there were a total of forty-nine Korean plants in Guatemala. AVANCSO, *El significado de la maquila*, 37.

22. Human Rights Watch, *From the Household to the Factory*, 57, 84–109, 129–132; VESTEX, "Directory of Manufacturers in Guatemala."

23. The cost of producing a man's sports shirt in Guatemala in 1987 was estimated to be $1.08 as compared to $2.02 in the United States and $1.48 in Hong Kong. AVANCSO, *El significado de la maquila*, 46 and 62–64.

24. Ibid., 79–80.

25. Bastos, *Poderes y quereres*, 49.

26. I am indebted to Deborah Levenson-Estrada's account of women unionists in the 1970s. Not only is her account one of the few studies of the period focusing on women, it is rich with the first-person accounts of workers (female and male) speaking about gender roles of the time. Levenson-Estrada, "Working-Class Feminism," 211. See also Levenson-Estrada's book, *Trade Unionists against Terror: Guatemala City, 1954–1985* (1994). Santiago Bastos argues that indigenous men and women have a different conception of masculinity and femininity that is centered in mutual responsibility; both are expected to work, and the family is jointly led by the two *jefes*. Bastos, *Poderes y quereres*, 79.

27. Bastos, *Poderes y quereres*, 51.

28. Levenson-Estrada, "Working-Class Feminism," 209.

29. Levenson-Estrada argues that "the line between 'protect' and 'possess' is thin" in the two cases that she relates (one of which is the Ray-O-Vac story repeated here). She ultimately argues that male unionists were helping and protecting their female co-workers and not trying to possess them as "*our* class's women." Levenson-Estrada, "Working-Class Feminism," 223.

30. Ibid.

31. Ibid., 224.

32. Ibid.

33. Levenson-Estrada relates an incident at the ACRICASA factory when management announced that only married women would be given Mother's Day off as a paid holiday. A group of workers argued with a manager inside his office, at which time one worker said, "If you don't give me this holiday because I am not a mother, I will lie on your desk and you bring a doctor in here to decide in front of everyone whether I am a mother." Accordingly, the embarrassed manager decided to give all mothers the paid holiday. Levenson-Estrada, "Working-Class Feminism," 218.

34. Ibid., 227.

35. Petersen, *Maquiladora Revolution*, 42.

36. Ibid.

37. Ibid., 42-43.

38. Red Centroamericana de Mujeres en Solidaridad con las Trabajadoras de Maquila, *Empleo sí, pero con dignidad* (Guatemala City, 1997). Quoted in Human Rights Watch, *From the Household to the Factory*, 84.

39. The *Código de Trabajo (Decreto 1441)* was initially passed in 1961 and then reformed several times, most notably in 2001 as part of the post-peace accords process. The Labor Code is available at http://www.legal.com.gt/leyes/doctos/work1/page_1.htm.

40. Petersen, *Maquiladora Revolution*, 41.

41. Mestiza women were the first employees of the *maquilas* in Guatemala, but today indigenous women are also joining the factory workforce. In addition, during the economic crisis at the turn of the millennium, men began to turn to the *maquilas* for employment in greater numbers. Human Rights Watch, *From the Household to the Factory*, 54.

42. Petersen, *Maquiladora Revolution*, 160.

43. The Phillips-Van Heusen plant, Camisas Modernas, was considered to be such a plant before it closed in 1998, soon after signing the first-ever collective bargaining agreement in an apparel *maquila* in Guatemala. U.S./Labor Education in the Americas Project, *Phillips-Van Heusen;* Petersen, *Maquiladora Revolution*, 40-50.

44. Some factories lock their doors during work hours, thus locking workers in and making it difficult for them to exit in case of an emergency. Petersen, *Maquiladora Revolution*, 69-71.

45. Regulations governing the factory owner's obligation to make health care available to employees is outlined in Article 61 of the *Código de Trabajo (Decreto 1441)*.

46. This Q420 includes the minimum wage of Q348 and the weekly seventh-day bonus on the completion of the week. This weekly bonus is set at a minimum of Q72 per month. Some *maquilas* calculate workers' salaries by the hour, and others do it by a complicated piece-rate value. Workers are also entitled to a yearly *aguinaldo* and the *bono 14*, each equal to one month's pay.

47. The Labor Code allows for a workweek of no more than forty-eight hours

if one adds the time allotted for breaks to the forty-two work hours. Night work hours are reduced to no more than six hours a night or at the most thirty-six hours a week. Guatemala, *Código de Trabajo (Decreto 1441)*, Chapter 3.

48. Guatemala, *Código de Trabajo (Decreto 1441)*, Articles 78, 127, 130.

49. Human Rights Watch, *From the Household to the Factory*, 86.

50. Ibid., 89.

51. Ibid., 93.

52. Ibid., 95.

53. Ibid., 106.

54. Guatemala, *Código de Trabajo (Decreto 1441)*, Article 151.

55. *Maquila* workers are entitled to health care through the IGSS. IGSS is supported through contributions made by the employer, the state, and the employee. Workers cannot partake of the free services of the IGSS, which are generally woefully inadequate in the first place, without their employer first registering them with the agency and supplying them with a work certification to prove employment status. *Maquila* employees report that employers often refuse or conveniently forget to perform the required tasks to register and certify their workers. Human Rights Watch, *From the Household to the Factory*, 102–103; Petersen, *Maquiladora Revolution*, Chapter 4.

56. Human Rights Watch, *From the Household to the Factory*, 108–109.

57. One of the stated goals of the Secretaría Presidencial de la Mujer is to require all government agencies to produce statistics according to sex. Caravantes, interview with the author, 26 November 2002.

58. AVANCSO, *El significado de la maquila en Guatemala*, 99.

59. Many supervisors are young South Koreans who are employed for only a short time in the Guatemalan factory and then return home; they work long hours, live and relax with other Koreans, and never learn more than a few words of Spanish and no indigenous languages.

60. They ridicule the Guatemalan worker by claiming that Korean workers work longer hours, never complain, and produce more rapidly.

61. Petersen, *Maquiladora Revolution*, 107.

62. Ibid., 117.

63. Although this is not necessarily the case in all Latin American countries where Solidarismo exists, in Guatemala, factory owners who encourage workers to reject unionization for Solidarismo dominate the Solidarismo movement. They contend that Solidarismo offers workers economic solutions to their economic problems in contrast to the inappropriate political solutions offered by other unions. Often the employer invests substantially in the organization initially but then cuts back, sometimes completely, once the independent union has been destroyed. Petersen, *Maquiladora Revolution*, 123–127.

64. Ibid., 105.

65. The Minister of Labor told Human Rights Watch that any independent in-

vestigation initiated by the agency had to first be approved by the minister. Human Rights Watch, *From the Household to the Factory*, 111.

66. Ibid., 112.

67. Pasquarella, "Historic Contract."

68. The section's budget was in fact reduced, from Q515,284 in 2002 to Q400,912 in 2003. Ministerio de Finanzas Públicas, *Presupuesto general . . . 2003;* Human Rights Watch, *From the Household to the Factory*, 114.

69. Ministerio de Finanzas Públicas, *Presupuesto general . . . 2003.*

70. Until 2000, workers were themselves responsible for taking their cases to court if they were not satisfied with the outcomes at the Ministry level. In 2000, however, the Procuraduría de Defensa del Trabajador was created within the Ministry to help provide workers with legal assistance for that purpose.

71. The Federation of Food and Allied Workers Union (Federación Sindical de Trabajadores de la Alimentación, Agro-Industrias y Similares; FESTRAS) started in the food industry but in 1996 began to expand into other sectors. In 1999, with the help of the AFL-CIO, the American NGO STITCH, and other smaller international groups, FESTRAS began to coordinate a campaign to organize workers in apparel and textile *maquilas*. This meant that FESTRAS had to train women organizers and address gender discrimination not only within the factory but also within the federation itself. One organizer, María Mejía, says, "Being in FESTRAS, it is a challenge to show even though I'm a woman, I can do the job." The internal adjustments have been difficult for the federation and are by no means complete. Connell, "Global Lessons in Guatemala."

72. AMES, GRUFEPROMEFAM, and CALDH all receive funding from international sources ranging from USAID to Oxfam Canada to Madre. Class, gender, and human rights are inseparably integrated in all of their campaigns. Rivas, interview with the author, 28 November 2002.

73. The Chief Executive Officer of PVH, Bruce Klatsky, consistently argued that the union had not met all the legal requirements for collective bargaining. After Human Rights Watch, of which Klatsky is a board member, confirmed that the union had indeed met the legal requirements, Klatsky agreed to allow PVH to negotiate. U.S./Labor Education in the Americas Project, *Phillips-Van Heusen.*

74. Ibid.

75. Human Rights Watch, *From the Household to the Factory*, 57.

76. Rivas, interview with the author, 28 November 2002.

77. In the spring of 2001, Armando de la Torre, the dean of the Graduate School of Social Sciences at the Universidad Francisco Marroquín in Guatemala City, criticized the U.S. government for pushing Guatemala for labor reforms to satisfy organized labor in its negotiations of CAFTA. He argued that the reforms would be detrimental for Guatemala, complaining that "apparently the future of Guatemala was the easiest 'bone' to throw." De la Torre, "Labor's Anti-Trade Drive."

78. Pasquarella, "Historic Contract."

79. White and Spieldoch, "Analysis of Free Trade Area."

80. This is clear from the experiences of Santiago Bastos as related in *Poderes y quereres* and confirmed by Tula Connell, "Global Lessons in Guatemala."

81. Rivas, interviews with the author, 22 May 1998 and 28 November 2002.

82. Levenson-Estrada, "Working-Class Feminism," 226.

CHAPTER 6. COUNTERING DISCOURSE: TOWARD RESISTANCE

1. "Women, organized and individually, marched this past June 29 (2004) in the capital city to renounce, once again, the growing wave of assassinations of Guatemalan women" (Asturias, "¡No más exterminio!").

2. NISGUA, "Guatemalan Elections Update."

3. Asturias, "Guatemala: Mujeres bajo acoso."

4. Peterson, cited in Young, "Masculinist Protection," 14.

5. Ibid., 3.

6. Ibid., 13.

7. Young argues that the Bush administration has portrayed itself as "the benign masculine protector"; its position as the protector with special knowledge of security necessitates the dependence of members of society and justifies its patriarchal right as the masculine protector keeping women (Muslim and Western) safe. Young, "Maculinist Protection," 9.

8. It is no coincidence that the theme of the first edition of the feminist newspaper *laCuerda* after the November 9, 2003, elections was "fears." Contributors wrote about fears of political violence, the manners in which political parties manipulated society's fears, fears of going against gender norms, and the attempts of social and political groups to silence women. *laCuerda 6, no. 62 (November 2003).*

9. Eleven presidential candidates participated in the November 2003 elections. The elections marked a significant strategic shift for Guatemalan elites in that "oligarchic interests have decided to enter the political arena themselves. Instead of simply supporting others, many of the country's most powerful families have surfaced to become candidates themselves" (Solano, "Three Decades Later," 1). Three candidates dominated the race by late October 2003: Oscar Berger Perdomo, supported by the Alianza GANA (Gran Alianza Nacional); Alvaro Colóm Caballeros, of the Unidad Nacional de la Esperanza (National Unity for Hope; UNE); and Efraín Ríos Montt, backed by the ruling FRG. Only one of the candidates, Colóm Caballeros, had accepted and incorporated the political agenda named "Mujeres en la diversidad," put forth by the women's movement. Berger Perdomo, the former candidate for Partido Avanzando Nacional (National Advancement Party; PAN) in the 1999 elections, is a lawyer and the former mayor of Guatemala City (1991-1999). His law partner had been Rodolfo Sosa de León, president of Basic Resource, an oil company that received questionable and profitable contracts in the Petén. Colóm Caballeros, considered a bit more liberal than

Berger Perdomo, had been a former Vice Minister of the Economy and director of the National Peace Fund (FONAPAZ), but was also a member of VESTEX and of a committee called MEGATEX, which helped to develop *maquila* projects and contracts. Thus both candidates had close connections to business and export production. Although neither Berger Perdomo nor Colóm Caballeros had any direct personal connections to the counterinsurgency, leaders in both parties did. The FRG, however, had the strongest links with Guatemala's dirty war: Ríos Montt had been the military head of state during what is considered the most repressive period in the army's counterinsurgency (1982–1983), and numerous other important FRG members were retired military officers who had participated in the counterinsurgency. Ríos Montt had tried to run for president in two previous elections, but the Corte de Constitucionalidad (CC) had ruled both times that he was ineligible under Article 186 of the Guatemalan Constitution, which forbids any participant in a coup (and their relatives to specified grades of removal) from being presidential or vice-presidential candidates (Amnesty International, "Guatemala: Legitimacy on the Line"). Barred from the presidency, Ríos Montt had run for Congress and risen to the presidency of the legislative body. From that post, and assisted by FRG-backed President Alfonso Portillo (1999–2003), the FRG packed the CC with Ríos Montt supporters, and after much debate between the CC and the Corte Suprema Justicia, it was decided that Article 186 did not apply to Ríos Montt because it was not in effect when he had led a coup in 1982. He was thus finally allowed to stand for president on the FRG ticket in the 2003 elections.

10. For instance, the party mobilized ex–Civil Patrol (PAC) members who had benefited in small ways from the dirty war to stage strategic political disruptions in favor of Ríos Montt's candidacy.

11. Ex-military officers from the authoritarian years are widely believed to be in charge of numerous organized crime rings involved with drug smuggling and other illegal activities. Solano, "Three Decades Later," 2–3.

12. They are taunting Menchú to "Go back to selling tomatoes in La Terminal [the central market in Guatemala City]." Pérez, "Agreden a Rigoberta Menchú."

13. In the *Leviathan* (1651, chap. 13, par. 9), the English philosopher Thomas Hobbes presents a bleak view of life in the state of nature (before government) as "nasty, brutish, and short." According to Hobbes, fears of violence lead individuals to enter into a contract with an absolutist state, granting the monarch complete powers in exchange for protection.

14. In fact, Ríos Montt had claimed that neither he nor the party would be able to control the anger of his supporters if his petition was denied ("Puede ocurrir que la dirección y los cuadros del partido no estén en condiciones de controlar a sus simpatizantes"). Amnesty International, "Guatemala: Legitimacy on the Line."

15. An examination of the political pamphlets distributed by the three frontrunners showed that all three spoke about curbing the rising violence against

women, but only Colóm Caballeros' literature directly addressed women's concerns, though it did so in a rather traditional way by stating that the presidential candidate promised "atención especial a grupos vulnerables (mujeres, niñez, juventud, tercera edad)" [special attention for vulnerable groups—women, children, young people, and elderly].

16. María Eugenia Solís García argues that the PAN tried to increase fear in the capital city during the preelectoral period by constantly discussing the rise of urban gangs and attributing insecurity to gang-related violence. She maintains that the focus on urban gangs was a calculated attempt to "criminalize the poor" to obtain the "fear" vote of the middle and upper classes ("Mensajes nefastos de campaña.")

17. Balboa, "En Guatemala el sistema político está colapsado."

18. MINUGUA, *Informes del Secretario General.*

19. Amnesty International, "Guatemala: Legitimacy on the Line."

20. For a discussion about memory and repression, see Jelin, *State Repression and the Labors of Memory* (2003).

21. Lamb, "Constructing the Victim," 108.

22. Arturo Escobar and others have insightfully discussed the power of labels. Escobar maintains that "labels determine access to resources, so that people must adjust to such categorization to be successful in their deals with the institution. A key mechanism at work here is that the whole reality of a person's life is reduced to a single feature or trait . . . in other words, the person is turned into a 'case'" (*Encountering Development,* 110).

23. Lamb, "Constructing the Victim," 118.

24. Ibid.

25. See Arias, *The Rigoberta Menchú Controversy* (2001), and Stoll, *Rigoberta Menchú and the Story of All Poor Guatemalans* (1999).

26. Enloe, "Dismantling Militarism," 29.

27. Lamb, "Constructing the Victim," 131.

28. Jelin, *State Repression and the Labors of Memory,* 72–73.

29. The origin of the Women in Development (WID) approach is often dated to the publication of Esther Boserup's seminal study, *Women's Role in Economic Development* (1970), which examined the destructive impacts of excluding women from development projects and decision making. The WID perspective advocated bringing women into development or mainstreaming women on equal terms with men. In the late 1970s and early 1980s, WID complemented equity discourse with an antipoverty approach that stressed income-generation strategies and skill development for women. In the mid-1980s, WID turned to an efficiency model, maintaining that development would be more efficient "if women's resources were utilized in full" and thus making women's economic participation synonymous with gender equity. By the second half of the 1970s, an alternative to WID, in the form of Women and Development (WAD), had taken shape. Informed by Marxist feminism, WAD focused not only on the integration of women into development

but on power relations between northern and southern nations. Consequently, WAD advocates such as Development Alternatives with Women for a New Era (DAWN) argued the importance of Third World women organizing themselves into autonomous women's organizations to first formulate and then obtain the fulfillment of their needs. In the 1990s, the World Bank, International Monetary Fund, state policy makers, and many nongovernmental organizations adopted a Gender and Development (GAD) approach. GAD goals usually include bringing women into the development process but also look at ways in which development can be used to transform unequal social/gender relations and empower women. Reproductive health initiatives have been one policy highlighted by the GAD approach. As we have seen, however, GAD proponents often use the concept of gender in reductionist ways, ignoring the larger contexts of socioeconomic and political relations within which gender and gender inequity and resistance are framed. As one group of scholars confirms, "Indeed the use of a narrow, rigid understanding of gender, despite their seeming focus on the inequality generated within notions of masculinity and femininity, can lead to an overemphasis on structures and institutions at the expense of seeing the agency of women, an agency that may not just perpetuate inequalities but also challenge them" (Bhavnani, Foran, and Kurian, "Introduction," 1-6).

30. Porter, "Caught in the Web?" 1.

31. Sonia Alvarez notes that similar changes accompanied globalization regionally: "Changing international donor and development policies, together with structural adjustment and the growing erasure of local states from the realm of social policy, may be propelling states and intergovernmental organizations (IGOs) to turn to some feminist NGOs as 'experts on gender' rather than as citizens' groups advocating on behalf of women's rights. Governments and IGOs increasingly seek out the more professionalized sectors of the feminist field to evaluate 'state policies with a gender perspective' and execute targeted social service and training (*capacitación*) programs for 'at risk' poor and working-class women— potentially distancing NGOs from their key societal constituencies, compromising their ability to critically monitor policy and advocate for more through-going (perhaps more feminist?) reform" ("Advocating Feminism," 1-2).

32. Porter and Verghese, "Falling between the Gaps," 137.

33. Audre Lorde maintained that "the master's tools will never dismantle the master's house" (*Sister Outsider*, 110-113).

34. Alvarez, Dagnino, and Escobar, "Latin American Social Movements," 18.

BIBLIOGRAPHY

PRIMARY SOURCES

Acevedo, Claudia, and Samantha Sams. "Editorial." *Identidades: Lesbianas guatemaltecas en su diversidad* 1 (July 2000): 3.

Ackerly, Brooke. "Book Reviews." *Signs* 29, no. 1 (Autumn 2003): 249.

Acosta-Belen, Edna, and Christine E. Bose, eds. *Researching Women in Latin America and the Caribbean.* Boulder, CO: Westview Press, 1993.

Agosín, Marjorie, ed. *Women, Gender, and Human Rights: A Global Perspective.* New Brunswick, NJ: Rutgers University Press, 2001.

Agrupación de Mujeres Tierra Viva, ed. *Conversario sobre avances, limitaciones y propuestas que, como mujeres, encontramos para el ejercicio de nuestro derecho de la salud.* Guatemala City: Agrupación de Mujeres Tierra Viva, 2002.

———. *El feminismo una opción de vida para las mujeres.* Guatemala City: Agrupación de Mujeres Tierra Viva, 2001.

———. *Lo que siempre quisiste saber sobre feminismo en Centroamérica y no te atreviste a preguntar.* Guatemala City: Agrupación de Mujeres Tierra Viva, 1994.

———. *Poder, liderazgo y participación política de las mujeres.* Guatemala City: Agrupación de Mujeres Tierra Viva, 1996.

———. *V informe hemerográfico 1996.* Guatemala City: Agrupación de Mujeres Tierra Viva, 1997.

Aguilar, Ana Leticia, et al., eds. *Movimiento de mujeres en Centroamérica.* Managua, Nicaragua: Programa Regional La Corriente, 1997.

Aguilera Peralta, Gabriel, Jorge Solares, René Poitevin, and Braulia Thillet de Solórzano. *Los problemas de la democracia.* Guatemala City: Facultad Latinoamericana de Ciencias Sociales, 1997.

Alarcón Alba, Angélica. *Diagnostic Study of the Guatemalan Women's Movement and Its Experiences in Political Advocacy.* 3 January 2003. http://www.wola.org/advocacy_training/atp_pubs_diagnostic_womens_movement_guatemala.htm.

Altman, Dennis. "Rupture or Continuity? The Internationalization of Gay Identities." *Social Text* 0, no. 48 (Autumn 1996): 77–94.

Alvarez, Sonia. "Advocating Feminism: The Latin American NGO Boom." *Global Solidarity Dialogue.* 20 January 2003, http://www.antenna.nl/~waterman/alvarez2.html.

————. *Engendering Democracy in Brazil: Women's Movements in Transition Politics*. Princeton, NJ: Princeton University Press, 1990.

Alvarez, Sonia, Evelina Dagnino, and Arturo Escobar. "The Cultural and the Political in Latin American Social Movements." In *Cultures of Politics/Politics of Cultures*, edited by Sonia Alvarez, Evelina Dagnino, and Arturo Escobar, 1–29. Boulder, CO: Westview Press, 1998.

America's Watch. *Guatemala: The Group for Mutual Support*. New York: America's Watch Committee, 1985.

Amnesty International. "Guatemala: Legitimacy on the Line: Human Rights and the 2003 Guatemalan Elections." 9 September 2003, http://web.amnesty.org/library/index/ENGAMR340512003.

Aranda, Josefina, Carlota Botey, and Rosario Robles. *Tiempo de crisis, tiempo de mujeres*. Oaxaca, Mexico: Universidad Autónoma "Benito Juárez" de Oaxaca, 2000.

Arias, Arturo, ed. *The Rigoberta Menchú Controversy*. Minneapolis, MN: University of Minneapolis Press, 1999.

Aron, Adrianne, Shawn Corne, Anthea Fursland, and Barbara Zelwer. "The Gender-Specific Terror of El Salvador and Guatemala: Post-traumatic Stress Disorder of Central American Refugee Women." *Women's Studies International Forum* 14, no. 1–2 (1991): 37–47.

Arriola, Aura Marina. *Ese obstinado sobrevivir: Autoetnografía de una mujer guatemalteca*. Guatemala City: Ediciones del Pensativo, 2000.

Asociación para el Avance de las Ciencias Sociales en Guatemala (AVANCSO). *El significado de la maquila en Guatemala: Elementos para su comprensión*. Guatemala City: AVANCSO, 1994.

Asturias, Laura. "Guatemala: Aprueban Ley de Desarrollo Social." *Tertulia* 4, no. 40 (29 September 2001). http://www.la-tertulia.net.

————. "Guatemala: Mujeres bajo acoso." *Tertulia* 6, no. 30 (21 October 2003). http://www.la-tertulia.net.

————. "¡No más exterminio!" *laCuerda* 7, no. 69 (July 2004). http://www.geocities.com/lacuerda_gt.

Balboa, Juan. "En Guatemala el sistema político está colapsado, asegura Nineth Montenegro." *La Jornada*, 17 November 2003, received from Bob Trudeau, rtrudeau@providence.edu.

Balderston, Daniel, and Donna J. Guy, eds. *Sex and Sexuality in Latin America*. New York: New York University Press, 1997.

Barrios-Klée, Walda, and Edda Gaviola Artigas. *Mujeres mayas y cambio social*. Guatemala City: Facultad Latinoamericana de Ciencias Sociales, 2001.

Bastos, Santiago. *Poderes y quereres: Historias de género y familia en los sectores populares de la ciudad de Guatemala*. Guatemala City: Facultad Latinoamericana de Ciencias Sociales, 2000.

Basu, Amrita. *The Challenge of Local Feminisms*. Boulder, CO: Westview Press, 1995.

Batliwala, Srilatha. "The Meaning of Women's Empowerment: New Concepts for Action." In *Population Policies Reconsidered: Health Empowerment and Rights,* edited by Gita Sen, Adrienne Germain, and Lincoln C. Chen, 127–138. Cambridge, MA: Harvard University Press, 1994.

Bayes, Jane H., Mary E. Hawkesworth, and Rita Mae Kelly. "Globalization, Democratization, and Gender Regimes." In *Gender, Globalization, and Democratization,* edited by Jane H. Bayes, Mary E. Hawkesworth, and Rita Mae Kelly, 1–14. Lanham, MD: Rowman and Littlefield, 2001.

Bergerson, Suzanne. "Political Economy Discourses of Globalization and Feminist Politics." *Signs* 26, no. 4 (Summer 2001): 983–1006.

Bhavnani, Kum-Kum, John Foran, and Priya Kurian. "An Introduction to Women, Culture and Development." In *Feminist Futures: Re-imagining Women, Culture and Development,* ed. Kum-Kum Bhavnani, John Forna, and Priya Kurian, 1–6. London: Zed Books, 2003.

Black, George. *Garrison Guatemala.* London: Zed Books, 1984.

Blacklock, Cathy. "Democratization and Popular Women's Political Organizations." CERLAC Working Papers Series North York, Ontario: York University, January 1999.

Blackwood, Evelyn. "Culture and Women's Sexualities." *Journal of Social Issues* 56, no. 2 (2000): 223–238.

Blackwood, Evelyn, and Saskia E. Wieringa, eds. *Same-Sex Relations and Female Desires: Transgender Practices across Cultures.* New York, NY: Columbia University Press, 1999.

Boserup, Esther. *Women's Role in Economic Development.* London: Allen & Unwinn, 1970.

Burgos Debray, Elizabeth, ed. *I, Rigoberta Menchú.* London: Verso, 1984.

Caba, Engracia Reyna. *KAL B'OP: Relato testimonial.* Guatemala City: Unidad Revolucionaria Nacional de Guatemala, 2001.

Cabarrús, Carolina, Dorotea Gómez, and Ligia González. *Y nos saltamos las trancas: Los cambios en la vida de las mujeres refugiadas retornadas guatemaltecas.* Guatemala City: Consejería en Proyectos, n.d.

Cabrera Pérez-Armiñán, María Luisa. *Tradicion y cambio de la mujer k'iche'.* Guatemala City: Instituto para el Desarrollo Económico Social de América Central (IDESAC), 1992.

Calderón, René, "How to Be a Lesbian in Guatemala." *theGully.com,* 16 October 2000. http://www.thegully.com/essays/gaymundo/001016acevedo.html. Interview with Claudia Acevedo.

Cohen, Jean, and Andrew Arato. *Civil Society and Political Theory.* Cambridge, MA: MIT Press, 1992.

Cohn, Carol, and Cynthia Enloe, "A Conversation with Cynthia Enloe: Feminists Look at Masculinity and the Men Who Wage War." *Signs* 28, no. 4 (Summer 2003): 1187–1207.

Colom, Yolanda. *Mujeres en la alborada: Guerrilla y participación femenina en Guatemala, 1973-1978.* Guatemala City: Artemis & Edinter, 1998.

Comisión de la Mujer, el Menor y la Familia del Congreso de la República de Guatemala. *Conociendo la ley para prevenir, sancionar y erradicar la violencia intrafamiliar.* Guatemala City: Comisión de la Mujer, el Menor y la Familia, 1997.

Connell, Tula. "Global Lessons in Guatemala." *http://www.aflcio.org/aboutaflcio/magazine/guatemala.cfm.*

Constitución Política de la República de Guatemala (31 May 1985). Guatemala City: Jimenez & Ayala, n.d.

Craske, Nikki. *Women and Politics in Latin America.* New Brunswick, NJ: Rutgers University Press, 1999.

Dagnino, Evelina. "Citizenship in Latin America." *Latin American Perspectives* 30, no. 2 (March 2003): 3-17.

Dary Fuentes, Claudia. *Mujeres tradicionales y nuevos cultivos.* Guatemala City: Facultad Latinoamericana de Ciencias Sociales, 1991.

Deere, Carmen Diana, and Magdalena León. *Mujer y tierra en Guatemala.* Guatemala City: AVANCSO, 1999.

De la Torre, Armando. "Labor's Anti-Trade Drive Claims a Victim, Guatemala." *Wall Street Journal,* 18 May 2001, http://www.ufm.edu.gt/debate/adlt.htm.

Del Cid Vargas, Paula Irene. "Estrategias para erradicar la violencia contra las mujeres." *laCuerda* 0, no. 7 (28 October 1998): 3. http://www.geocities.com/lacuerda_gt.

Delgado, Luz Marina. *Manos de mujer.* Great Falls, VA: La Ruta Maya Conservation Foundation, 1996.

D'Emilio, John. "Capitalism and Gay Identity: The Gender Sexuality Reader: Cultural History, Political Economy." In *The Gender Sexuality Reader: Culture, History, and Political Economy,* edited by Roger Lancaster and Micaela de Leonardo, 169-178. New York: Routledge, 1997.

Dore, Elizabeth, ed. *Gender Politics in Latin America: Debates in Theory and Practice.* New York: Monthly Review Press, 1997.

Enloe, Cynthia. "Demilitarization—or More of the Same? Feminist Questions to Ask in the Postwar Moment." In *The Postwar Moment: Militaries, Masculinities and International Peacekeeping,* edited by Cynthia Cockburn and Dubravka Zarkov, 22-32. London: Lawrence & Wishart, 2002.

Escobar, Arturo. *Encountering Development: The Making and Unmaking of the Third World.* Princeton, NJ: Princeton University Press, 1995.

Escobar, Arturo, and Sonia Alvarez, eds. *The Making of Social Movements in Latin America: Identity, Strategy, and Democracy.* Boulder, CO: Westview Press, 1992.

Escobar Sarti, Carolina. *Palabras sonámbulas.* Guatemala City: Ediciones Papiro, 2000.

———. "Women You Don't Hear." In *Palabras sonámbulas*. Guatemala City: Ediciones CES, 2000.

Expresiones Organizadas de Mujeres de la Sociedad. *Plataforma política para el desarrollo de las mujeres guatemaltecas*. Guatemala City: Sector de Mujeres, 1999.

Fallon, Kathleen M. "Transforming Women's Citizenship Rights within an Emerging Democratic State: The Case of Ghana." *Gender & Society* 17, no. 4 (August 2003): 525–543.

Fisher, Julie. *Nongovernments: NGOs and the Political Development of the Third World*. West Hartford, CT: Kumarian Press, 1998.

Franco, Jean. *Plotting Women: Gender and Representation in Mexico*. New York: Columbia University Press, 1989.

Freeman, Carla. "Is Local : Global as Feminine : Masculine? Rethinking the Gender of Globalization." *Signs* 26, no. 4 (Summer 2001): 1007–1037.

FUNDESA, *Business Guidebook*. http://www.quetzalnet.com/quetzalnet/Bus_Guide.html.

Gabriel Xiquín, Calixta. *Tejiendo los sucesos en el tiempo*. Rancho Palos Verdes, CA: Yax Te' Foundation, 2002.

Gaspar de Alba, Alicia. "Descarada/No Shame: A[bridged] Politics of Location." In *The Wild Good: Lesbian Photographs and Writings about Love*, edited by Beatrix Gates, 217–223. New York: Anchor Books, 1996. Reprinted in Alicia Gaspar de Alba, *La Llorona on the Longfellow Bridge: Poetry y Otras Movidas*. Houston, Texas: Arte Público Press, 2003, 85–92.

Gehlert Mata, Carlos. *Vida, enfermedad y muerte en Guatemala*. Guatemala City: Editorial Universitaria de Guatemala, n.d.

Gellert, Gisela, and Silvia Irene Palma C. *Precariedad urbana, desarrollo comunitario y mujeres en el área metropolitana de Guatemala*. Guatemala City: Facultad Latinoamericana de Ciencias Sociales, 1999.

Green, Linda. *Fear as a Way of Life: Mayan Widows in Rural Guatemala*. New York: Columbia University Press, 1999.

Guatemala, Government of. *Código Civil (1963)*. Guatemala City: N.d.

———. *Código de Trabajo (Decreto 1441)* (1961; rev. 2001). Guatemala City: N.d.

———. *Ley de desarrollo social (Decreto 42-2001)*. Guatemala City: N.d.

———. *Ley para prevenir, sancionar y erradicar la violencia intrafamiliar (Decreto 97-96)*. Guatemala City: Don Carlos, 2002.

Guatemala: La fuerza incluyente del desarrollo humano. Guatemala City: Sistema de Naciones Unidas en Guatemala, 2000.

Harbury, Jennifer. *Bridge of Courage: Life Stories of the Guatemalan Compañeros and Compañeras*. Monroe, ME: Common Courage Press, 1994.

Hawkesworth, Mary. "Confounding Gender." *Signs* 22, no. 3 (Spring 1997): 649–686.

Hobbes, Thomas. *Leviathan*. Chapter 13, paragraph 9. N.p., 1651.

Hooks, Margaret. *Guatemalan Women Speak*. London: Catholic Institute for International Relations, 1991.

Hooper, Charlotte. "Masculinities in Transition: The Case of Globalization." In *Global Restructuring: Sightings, Sites and Resistances,* edited by Marianne H. Marchand and Anne Sisson Runyan, 59–73. London: Routledge, 2000.

Human Rights Watch. *From the Household to the Factory: Sex Discrimination in the Guatemalan Labor Force.* New York: Human Rights Watch, January 2002.

Identidades: Lesbianas guatemaltecas en su diversidad (Guatemala City) 1, no. 00 (July 2000).

Iglesia Noruega, ed. *Por favor, nunca más: Testimonio de mujeres, víctimas del conflicto armado en Guatemala.* Guatemala City: Iglesia Noruega, 1997.

Instituto Interamericano de Derechos Humanos (IIDH) and Comité de América Latina y el Caribe para la Defensa de los Derechos Humanos de la Mujer. *Protección internacional de los derechos humanos de las mujeres: I curso taller.* San José, Costa Rica: IIDH, 1997.

Instrumentos de derechos humanos de protección de la mujer. Guatemala City: Cooperación Comunidad Europea, n.d.

Jaquette, Jane, ed. *The Women's Movement in Latin America: Feminism and the Transition to Democracy.* Boulder, CO: Westview Press, 1991.

Jelin, Elizabeth. "Citizenship and Alterity: Tensions and Dilemmas." *Latin American Perspectives* 30, no. 2 (March 2003): 101–117.

———. "Engendering Human Rights." In *Gender Politics in Latin America,* edited by Elizabeth Dore, 65–83. New York: Monthly Review Press, 1997.

———. *State Repression and the Labors of Memory.* Minneapolis, MN: University of Minnesota Press, 2003.

———, ed. *Women and Social Change in Latin America.* London: Zed Books, 1990.

Jonasdottir, Anna. "On the Concept of Interests, Women's Interests, and the Limitations of Interest Theory." In *The Political Interests of Gender,* edited by K. B. Jones and Anna Jonasdottir, 33–65. London: Sage, 1998.

Kabeer, Naila. "Conflicts over Credit: Re-evaluating the Empowerment of Loans to Women in Rural Bangladesh." *World Development* 29, no. 1 (2001): 63–84.

Küppers, Gaby, ed. *Compañeras: Voices from the Latin American Women's Movement.* London: Latin American Bureau, 1994.

Lamb, Sharon, ed. *New Versions of Victims: Feminists Struggle with the Concept.* New York: New York University Press, 1999.

Lancaster, Roger N., and Micaela de Leonardo, eds. *The Gender Sexuality Reader: Culture, History, and Political Economy.* New York: Routledge, 1997.

Levenson-Estrada, Deborah. "The Loneliness of Working-Class Feminism: Women in the 'Male World' of Labor Unions, Guatemala City, 1970s." In *The Gendered World[s?] of Latin American [women?] Workers,* ed. John D. French and Daniel James, 208–231. Durham, NC: Duke University Press, 1997.

———. *Trade Unionists against Terror: Guatemala City, 1954–1985.* Chapel Hill, NC: University of North Carolina Press, 1994.

Lewin, Ellen, and William L. Leap, eds. *Out in Theory: The Emergence of Lesbian and Gay Anthropology.* Urbana, IL: University of Illinois Press, 2002.

López Sologaistoa, Jorge. "Guatemala: Portrait of an Activist." *theGully .com*, 30 October 2000. http://www.thegully.com/essays/gaymundo/001030 portrait.html.

Lorde, Audre. *Sister Outsider: Essays and Speeches.* Freedom, CA: The Crossing Press, 1984.

MacNabb, Valerie. "Guatemalan Women and the Struggle for Political Transition." Ph.D. diss., University of Toronto, 2003.

Majawil Q'ij., Ukux Ulew, Defensoría de la Mujer Maya, Asociación de Mujeres Nuevo Amanecer. *Decreto Gubernativo 97-96: Ley para prevenir, sancionar y erradicar la violencia intrafamiliar.* Guatemala City: UNIFEM, 2002.

———. *Reformas constitucionales.* N.p., n.d.

Marchand, Marianne H., and Anne Sisson Runyan, eds. *Gender and Global Restructuring: Sightings, Sites and Resistances.* London: Routledge, 2000.

Marchand, Marianne H., and Anne Sisson Runyan. "Introduction: Feminist Sightings of Global Restructuring: Conceptualizations and Reconceptualizations." In *Gender and Global Restructuring: Sightings, Sites and Resistances,* ed. Marianne H. Marchand and Anne Sisson Runyan, 1–25. London: Routledge, 2000.

Markowitz, Lisa, and Karen W. Tice. "Paradoxes of Professionalization: Parallel Dilemmas in Women's Organizations in the Americas." *Gender & Society* 16, no. 6 (December 2002): 941–958.

Marroquín, Maria Dolores. "Cumplimiento de los acuerdos de paz en lo relativo a las mujeres existen avances?" *Ut'z'ilal': Organo informativo Asamblea de la Sociedad Civil,* no. 2 (29 December 1997): 9.

Marshall, Thomas Humphrey. *Citizenship and Social Class.* Cambridge, UK: Cambridge University Press, 1950.

Martin, Biddy. "Extraordinary Homosexuals and the Fear of Being Ordinary." In *Feminism Meets Queer Theory,* edited by Elizabeth Reed and Naomi Schor, 109–135. Bloomington, IN: Indiana University Press, 1997.

Mattson, Corey (updated by Marie Ayer). "The Maquila in Guatemala: Facts and Trends." *STITCH Online: Organizers for Labor Justice,* http://www .stitchonline.org/archives/maquila.html.

McClure, Heather H. "Sexuality, Power, and Performance in Guatemala and the United States Asylum Law." Ph.D. diss., Northwestern University, 1999.

Menchú, Rigoberta. *Rigoberta: La nieta de los mayas.* Madrid: Aguilar, 1998.

Méndez de la Vega, Luz. *Mujer, desnudez y palabras.* Guatemala City: Artemis Edinter, 2002.

Mijangos, Eugenia. "La organización de género y sus perspectivas." *Debate* 1, no. 4 (6 January 1997): 29.

Ministerio de Finanzas Públicas. *Presupuesto general de ingresos y egresos del estado del ejercicio fiscal 2003.* http://www.minfin.gob.gt.

MINUGUA. *Los desafíos para la participación de las mujeres guatemaltecas.* Guatemala City: MINUGUA, n.d.

———. *Informes del Secretario General, MINUGUA 2002-2003.* http://www .minugua.guate.net/Informes/INFOCRONOG/CRONOG.html.

———. "Interview with Lili Caravantes, Secretaría Presidencial de la Mujer." *Crónicas de MINUGUA y Sistema Naciones Unidas* 57 (21 March 2002): 4-5.

———. "Una mirada a los compromisos relativos a las mujeres en los acuerdos de paz." *Crónicas de MINUGUA y Sistema Naciones Unidas* 57 (21 March 2002): 1-2.

Mogrovejo, Norma. *Un amor que se atrevió a decir su nombre: La lucha de las lesbianas y su relación con los movimientos homosexual y feminista en América Latina.* Mexico City: Centro de Documentación de la Mujer y Archivo Histórico Lésbico (CDAHL), 2000.

———. "Sexual Preferences, the Ugly Duckling of Feminist Demands: The Lesbian Movement in Mexico." In *Same-Sex Relations and Female Desires: Transgender Practices across Cultures,* edited by Evelyn Blackwood and Saskia E. Wieringa, 308-335. New York: Columbia University Press, 1999.

Mohanty, Chandra Talpade. *Feminism without Borders: Decolonizing Theory, Practicing Solidarity.* Durham, NC: Duke University Press, 2003.

Molyneux, Maxine. "Analyzing Women's Movements." *Development and Change* 29, no. 2 (1998): 219-245.

Monzón, Ana Silvia. "Rasgos históricos de la exclusión de las mujeres en Guatemala." *Cuadernos de desarrollo humano,* no. 2001-2006 (2001): 1-28.

Morris, Rosalind C. "Educating Desire: Thailand, Transnationalism, and Transgression." *Social Text* 15, nos. 3-4 (Fall/Winter 1997): 53-79.

Moser, Caroline, and Cathy McIlwaine. *La violencia en el contexto del posconflicto: Según la percepción de comunidades urbanas pobres de Guatemala.* Washington, D.C.: World Bank, 2001.

Murray, Stephen. *Latin American Male Homosexualities.* Albuquerque: University of New Mexico Press, 1995.

Network in Solidarity with the People of Guatemala (NISGUA). "Guatemalan Elections Update." November 2003. http://www.nisgua.org.

Oficina Nacional de la Mujer and Proyecto Mujer y Reformas Jurídicas. *Las obligaciones legislativas a factor de las mujeres derivadas de los acuerdos de paz.* Guatemala City: Proyecto Mujer y Reformas Jurídicas, 1997.

———. *Proyecto de Ley Orgánica del Instituto Nacional de la Mujer.* N.p., n.d.

Pape Yalibat, Edgar, Elizabeth Quiroa, and Sofía Vásquez. *Contribuciones ocultas de las mujeres a la economía.* Guatemala City: Facultad Latinoamericana de Ciencias Sociales, 2001.

Pasquarella, Jennie. "Historic Contract Signed by Guatemalan Maquila Workers." *Sweatshopwatch.org,* 11 August 2003. http://www.sweatshopwatch .org/headlines/2003/choi_aug03.html.

Pepper, David. *Eco-Socialism: From Deep Ecology to Social Justice.* London: Routledge, 1993.

Pérez, Sonia. "Agreden a Rigoberta Menchú: Turbas del FRG atacan a Premio Nobel en diligencia judicial en la CC." *Prensa Libre,* 10 October 2003, http://www.prensalibre.com/pl/2003/octubre/10/69723/html.

Petersen, Kurt. *The Maquiladora Revolution in Guatemala.* New Haven, CT: Orville H. Schell, Jr., Center for International Human Rights at Yale Law School, 1992.

Petrich, Perla, ed. *Vida de las mujeres del Lago de Atitlán.* Guatemala City: IRIPAZ, 1996.

Pile, Steve. "Introduction: Opposition, Political Identities and Spaces of Resistance." In *Geographies of Resistance,* edited by Steve Pile and Michael Keith, 1-32. London: Routledge, 1997.

Porter, Fenella, and Valsa Verghese. "Falling between the Gaps." In *Feminists Doing Development,* ed. Marilyn Porter and Ellen Judd, 137. London: Zed Books, 1999.

Porter, Marilyn. "Caught in the Web? Feminists Doing Development." In *Feminists Doing Development,* ed. Marilyn Porter and Ellen Judd, 1-14. London: Zed Books, 1999.

Porter, Marilyn, and Ellen Judd, eds. *Feminists Doing Development.* London: Zed Books, 1999.

"Presidente convocó el Consejo Nacional de Desarrollo Urbano y Rural." *Diario La Hora,* 20 November 2001, sec. A.

Proyecto de ley orgánica del Instituto Nacional de la Mujer, INAM. Guatemala City: Ediciones y Servicios Librería e Imprenta, n.d.

Proyecto Mujer y Reformas Jurídicas. *Democracia y participación política de las mujeres en Guatemala.* 2nd ed. Guatemala City: XL Publicaciones, 1998.

———. *Estudio de factibilidad financiero institucional: Proyecto del Instituto Nacional de la Mujer, INAM.* Guatemala City: XL Publicaciones, 1999.

———. *Iniciativa de ley de creación del Instituto Nacional de la Mujer, INAM.* Guatemala City: XL Publicaciones, 1999.

Puwar, Nirmal. "Interview with Carole Pateman: The Sexual Contract, Women in Politics, Globalization and Citizenship." *Feminist Review* 70 (2002): 123-133.

Rai, Shirin M. *Gender and the Political Economy of Development.* Cambridge, UK: Polity Press, 2002.

Ramírez, Chiqui. *La Guerra de los 36 Años: Vista con ojos de mujer de la izquierda.* Guatemala City: Editorial Óscar de León Palacios, 2001.

Rosenbaum, Brenda. *With Our Heads Bowed: The Dynamics of Gender in a Maya Community.* Albany, NY: University of Albany, 1993.

Rummel, Inés. *Saliendo del closet.* 2nd ed. Guatemala City: Inés Rummel and Mujer-es Somos, 1997.

Ruthrauff, John, and Teresa Carlson. *A Guide to the Inter-American Development*

Bank and World Bank: Strategies for Guatemala 1997. Silver Spring, MD: Center for Democratic Education, 1997.

Salinas, Gilda. *Alaíde Foppa: El eco de tu nombre*. Miguel Hidalgo, Mexico: Editorial Grijalbo, 2002.

Sams, Samantha. "Lesbian Liberation: Part of a New Nation? Sexual Diversity in the Guatemalan Social Movement." *Report on Guatemala* 23, no. 2 (Summer 2002): 7–10.

Sanborn, Helen Josephine. "A Wellesley Graduate's Travels in Guatemala." In *Women through Women's Eyes: Latin American Women in Nineteenth-Century Travel Accounts*, edited by June E. Hahner, 157–173. Wilmington, DE: Scholarly Resources, 1998.

Sanford, Victoria. "From I, Rigoberta to the Commissioning of Truth: Maya Women and the Reshaping of Guatemalan History." *Cultural Critique* 47 (Winter 2001): 16–53.

Saunders, Kriemild, ed. *Feminist Post-Development Thought: Rethinking Modernity, Post-Colonialism and Representation*. London: Zed Books, 2002.

Schild, Veronica. " 'Gender Equity' without Social Justice: Women's Rights in the Neoliberal Age." *NACLA* 34, no. 1 (July/August 2000): 25–28.

———. "Neo-Liberalism's New Gendered Market Citizens: The Civilizing Dimension of Social Programmes in Chile." *Citizenship Studies* 4, no. 3 (2000): 275–305.

———. "New Subjects of Rights? Women's Movements and the Construction of Citizenship in the 'New Democracies.' " In *Cultures of Politics/Politics of Cultures*, edited by Sonia Alvarez, Evelina Dagnino, and Arturo Escobar, 93–117. Boulder, CO: Westview Press, 1998.

Schirmer, Jennifer. "The Seeking of Truth and the Gendering of Consciousness." In *Viva: Women and Popular Protest in Latin America*, edited by Sarah Radcliffe and Sallie Westwood, 30–64. London: Routledge, 1993.

———. " 'Those Who Die for Life Cannot Be Called Dead': Women and Human Rights Protests in Latin America." *Harvard Human Rights Yearbook* (1998): 41–76.

Sector de Mujeres. *Caminando hacia la institucionalización de políticas públicas para las mujeres guatemaltecas: Análisis comparativo entre el documento integrado y la propuesta del Consejo Consultivo y la del Foro Nacional de la Mujer*. Guatemala City: Imprenta Mercurio for the Sector de Mujeres, 2000.

———. *Ejerciendo nuestra ciudadanía desde la auditoria social de las mujeres: Primer informe sobre el funcionamiento de la Secretaría Presidencial de la Mujer y los avances de la política de desarrollo integral de las mujeres*. Guatemala City: Sector de Mujeres, 2001.

———. *Mujeres construyendo la paz*. Guatemala City: Programa de Mujeres, n.d.

"Sex Education Debate." *Mesoamérica* 20, no. 12 (December 2001): 2.

Sieder, Rachel. *Derecho consuetudinario y transición democrática en Guatemala*. Guatemala City: Facultad Latinoamericana de Ciencias Sociales, 1996.

Sieder, Rachel, Megan Thomas, George Vickers, and Jack Spence. *Who Governs? Guatemala Five Years after the Peace Accords.* Cambridge, MA: Hemisphere Initiatives, January 2002.

Simo, Ana. "Guatemala: Making an Oasis in a Culture of Violence." theGully .com, 23 October 2001. http:www.thegully.com/essays/gaymundo/001023 oasis.html.

Siu, Ivonne, ed. *Centroamérica: Las mujeres en el espacio local.* Managua, Nicaragua: Programa Regional La Corriente, 1997.

Slater, David. "Rethinking the Spatialities of Social Movements: Questions of (B)orders, Culture, and Politics in Global Times." In *Culture of Politics/Politics of Cultures,* edited by Sonia Alvarez, Evelina Dagino, and Arturo Escobar, 380–401. Boulder, CO: Westview Press, 1998.

Smith-Ayala, Emilie. *The Granddaughters of Ixmucané: Guatemalan Women Speak.* Toronto, Canada: Women's Press, 1991.

Solano, Luis. "Three Decades Later: Old and New Oligarchies, Military and Intelligence Networks of the Counterinsurgency Participate in the 2003 General Elections." *The Electoral Observer,* Bulletin No. 4 (October 2003): 1.

Solís García, María Eugenia. "Mensajes nefastos de campaña." *laCuerda* 6, no. 62 (November 2003). http://www.geocities.com/lacuerda_gt.

Soto, Max Alberto, Carlos Alberto Sevilla, and Charles R. Frank, Jr. *Guatemala: Desempleo y subempleo.* San José, Costa Rica: Editorial Universitaria Centroamericana, 1982.

Squires, Judith. *Gender in Political Theory.* Malden, MA: Polity Press, 1999.

Stein, Arlene. "Sisters and Queers: The Decentering of Lesbian Feminism." In *The Gender Sexuality Reader: Culture, History, Political Economy,* edited by Roger N. Lancaster and Micaela de Leonardo, 378–391. New York: Routledge, 1997.

Stephen, Lynn. "Anthropological Research on Latin American Women: Past Trends and New Directions for the 1990s." In *Researching Women in Latin America and the Caribbean,* edited by Edna Acosta-Belén and Christine E. Bose, 77–97. Boulder, CO: Westview Press, 1993.

———. *Women and Social Movements in Latin America: Power from Below.* Austin: University of Texas Press, 1997.

Stern, Richard. "Gay Life Emerges in Guatemala." *theGully.com.,* 16 October 2000. http://www.thegully.com/essays/gaymundo/001016gay_guat.html.

Stoll, David. *Rigoberta Menchú and the Story of All Poor Guatemalans.* Boulder, CO: Westview Press, 1999.

Stoltz Chinchilla, Norma. *Nuestras utopías: Mujeres guatemaltecas del siglo xx.* Guatemala City: Agrupación de Mujeres Tierra Viva, 1998.

Thillet de Solórzano, Braulia. *Mujeres y percepciones políticas.* Guatemala City: Facultad Latinoamericana de Ciencias Sociales, 2001.

Traub-Werner, Marion, and Lynda Yanz, eds. *Women behind the Labels: Worker*

Testimonies from Central America. Washington, D.C.: Maquila Solidarity Network and Support Team International for Textileras (STITCH), 2000.

UNIFEM-UNICEF. *Políticas públicas con perspectiva de género en Centroamérica.* Guatemala City: UNIFEM-UNICEF, 1994.

———. *El sexismo en los textos escolares en Centroamérica.* Guatemala City: UNIFEM-UNICEF, 1996.

United States Agency for International Development (USAID). "Guatemala." *http://www.usaid.gov/policy/budget/cbj2004/latin_america_caribbean/guatemala.pdf.*

U.S./Labor Education in the Americas Project. *Phillips-Van Heusen: An Industry "Leader" Unveiled.* 15 June 1999. http://www.usleap.org/Maquilas/PVHCampaign/PVHreport.html.

Valenzuela Sotomayor, María del Rosario. *Mujer y género en Guatemala: Magia y realidad.* Guatemala City: Artemis Editner, 2001.

Velásquez Nimatuj, Irmalicia. "Desigualdades de género y resistencia." *laCuerda* 4, no. 46 (June 2002): 10. http://www.geocities.com/lacuerda_gt.

VESTEX. "Directory of Manufacturers in Guatemala." http://www.apparel.com.gt.

———. "Guatemala Apparel and Textile Industry." http://www.apparel.com.gt.

———. "Investment Capital." http://www.apparel.com.gt.

Villaseñor Velarde, María Eugenia, et al. *Violencia doméstica y agresión social en Guatemala.* 2nd ed. Guatemala City: Fundación Friedrich Ebert, 1996.

Waylen, Georgina. "Gender, Feminism and the State: An Overview." In *Gender, Politics and the State,* edited by Vicky Randall and Georgina Waylen, 1–17. London: Routledge, 1998.

Weed, Elizabeth, and Naomi Schor, eds. *Feminism Meets Queer Theory.* Bloomington: Indiana University Press, 1997.

White, Marceline, and Alexandra Spieldoch. "Analysis of Free Trade Area of the Americas Text from a Gender Perspective." January 2003. http://www.stitchonline.org/archives.html.

Wiergna, Saskia. "Women's Interests and Empowerment: Gender Planning Reconsidered." *Development and Change* 25, no. 4 (1994): 829–848.

Young, Iris Marion. "The Logic of Masculinist Protection: Reflections on the Current Security State." *Signs* 29, no. 1 (Autumn 2003): 1–25.

Yúdice, George. "The Globalization of Culture and the New Civil Society." In *Culture of Politics/Politics of Culture,* edited by Sonia Alvarez, Evelina Dagnino, and Arturo Escobar, 353–379. Boulder, CO: Westview Press, 1998.

INTERVIEWS

Acevedo, Claudia (Co-founder, Lesbiradas). Interview with the author, Guatemala City, 27 November 2002.

Armas España, Malvina (Director, Proyecto Mujer y Reformas Jurídicas). Interview with the author, Guatemala City, 19 May 1998.

Asturias, Laura (Editor, *laCuerda*). Interview with the author, Guatemala City, 20 May 1998.

Caravantes, Lili (Secretaria, Secretaría Presidencial de la Mujer). Interview with the author, Guatemala City, 26 November 2002.

Cofiño, Ana María (Editor, *laCuerda*). Interview with the author, Guatemala City, 20 May 1998.

García Montenegro, Nineth (Chair, Comisión de la Mujer y la Familia del Congreso, member of the Foro Nacional de la Mujer, founder of Group for Mutual Support). Interview with the author, Guatemala City, 22 May 1998.

Lemus, Giovanna (Director, Grupo Guatemalteco de Mujeres). Interview with the author, Guatemala City, 20 May 1998.

López Sologaistoa, Jorge (President, Organización de Apoyo a una Sexualidad Integral frente al Sida, OASIS). Interview with the author, Guatemala City, 28 November 2002.

Morales Jorge, María (President, Majawil Q'ij). Interview with the author, Guatemala City, 27 November 2002.

Morán, Sandra (Sector de Mujeres). Interview with the author, Guatemala City, 18 May 1998.

Pellecer, Carmen Lucía (Co-Coordinator, Agrupación de Mujeres Tierra Viva). Interview with the author, Guatemala City, 19 May 1998 and 27 November 2002.

Ponce, Noraida (Co-Coordinator, Agrupación de Mujeres Tierra Viva). Interview with the author, Guatemala City, 27 November 2002.

Rivas, Olga (Coordinator, GRUFEPROMEFAM). Interviews with the author, Guatemala City, 22 May 1998 and 28 November 2002.

Rodríguez, Edna (Asistente Principal, Proyecto Mujer y Reformas Jurídicas and Convergencia Cívico Política de Mujeres). Interview with the author, Guatemala City, 19 May 1998.

Sánchez, Blanca (Director, FUNDAGUATE). Interview with the author, Guatemala City, 21 May 1998.

INDEX

nous citizens, 124n.26; and laws, 46, 51; and lesbians, 73–74; and local/global intersection, 63; social construction of, 21; and state repression, 26; and women in social movements, 24, 27

Feminists: and economic component of justice, 104; and Foro, 36, 117n.65; and gender discrimination, 44; and gendered violence, 98; and Guatemalan women's movement, 29–31, 33; influence in global restructuring, 13; and laws, 48, 53; and lesbians, 70, 73, 74, 122–123n.57; and *maquila* industry, 91; and Mexican lesbian movement, 64, 65, 121n.14; and neoliberal discourse, 4, 109n.11; of the North, 8, 10–11; popular feminists, 29, 77, 90; and Secretaría Presidencial de la Mujer, 55; and solidarity across borders, 7–8; of the South, 8, 10–11, 12; and transitional democracies, 41

Formal economy, 16, 20, 77, 83, 91, 96, 107

Foro Nacional de la Mujer (National Women's Forum; Foro), 35, 36–37, 38, 55, 56, 117n.65

Gay movement, 62, 64–68, 70, 71, 72, 122n.46

Gender and Development (GAD), 104, 119n.34, 130n.29

Gender discrimination: and capacity to reproduce, 77, 83; and Foro, 38; and Guatemalan women's movement, 30; and laws, 15, 20, 44, 50, 51, 57, 95; and *maquila* industry, 93; and peace accords, 44–45; and reproductive status, 86–88; and unions, 127n.71

Gendered violence: cooperative efforts against, 33; and indigenous women,

45–46, 102–103; and laws, 45, 46–48, 118n.9; and masculinist protection, 98–99, 100; and state, 26, 38, 47, 98. *See also* Domestic violence

Gender equality: and Guatemalan women's movement, 13, 14; and laws, 49, 51, 58; and peace accords, 35, 44–45

Gender equity: and citizenship, 5, 31, 42, 112n.5; and democratization, 42; and economic development, 55; and employment options and conditions, 1, 88, 107; and Foro, 37; and globalization, 2, 5; and Guatemalan women's movement, 1, 3, 27, 29–31; and laws, 46; and Mexican lesbian movement, 64; and peace accords, 35; and strategic interests, 9

Gender norms: and Catholic Church, 23–24, 30, 116n.50; and communism, 26, 115n.34; and employment options and conditions, 16, 20, 21, 51, 82, 84, 88–89, 95, 96, 107; and female-dominated workforces, 75; and lesbians, 70, 73–74; political implications of changing, 20, 22; and social movements, 25–26, 115n.33

Gender relations: and economic development, 119n.34; and employment options and conditions, 57–58, 77, 82–83; and Guatemalan women's movement, 2; and laws, 47, 51, 52

Gender roles: and Catholic Church, 23–24; and employment options and conditions, 77, 82–84, 95; and family, 23, 44, 50–51; and limitations on women, 24–26, 51, 83; and military state, 23, 27; and political violence, 99; reexamination of, 24, 83, 97; and state, 23, 39

Geographical location: and Foro, 37; and Guatemalan women's move-

U.S. Generalized System of Preferences, 94
US/Labor Education in the Americas Project, 93
U.S. Trade Representative, 91–92, 94

Wages, 86, 88, 104, 125n.46
Woc, Millie, 85

Women and Development (WAD), 104, 130–131n.29
Women in Development (WID), 54, 104, 119n.34, 130n.29
Women's Defense Program, 46

Young, Iris Marion, 98, 100, 128n.7